LAW AND LEGAL THEORY
IN ENGLAND AND AMERICA

Law and Legal Theory in England and America

RICHARD A. POSNER

CLARENDON PRESS · OXFORD
1996

Oxford University Press, Great Clarendon Street, Oxford OX2 6DP
Oxford New York
Athens Auckland Bangkok Bogota Bombay
Buenos Aires Calcutta Cape Town Dar es Salaam
Delhi Florence Hong Kong Istanbul Karachi
Kuala Lumpur Madras Madrid Melbourne
Mexico City Nairobi Paris Singapore
Taipei Tokyo Toronto
and associated companies in
Berlin Ibadan

Oxford is a trade mark of Oxford University Press

Published in the United States
by Oxford University Press Inc., New York

British Library Cataloguing in Publication Data
Data available

Library of Congress Cataloging in Publication Data
Data available
ISBN 0–19–826471–2

1 3 5 7 9 10 8 6 4 2

Typeset by Cambrian Typesetters, Frimley, Surrey
Printed in Great Britain on acid-free paper by
Bookcraft Ltd., Midsomer Norton, Avon

For Charlene

Preface

In October of last year I delivered three lectures at Oxford University, inaugurating the annual Clarendon Law Lectures series, sponsored by the Oxford University Press. In my lectures, of which this book is a revised version, I attempted a comparative analysis of the English and American legal systems. There is a considerable literature, illustrated by Atiyah and Summers's well-known book, on the subject,[1] and the contributors to that literature know far more than I about the English legal system. But my perspective differs from that of the previous contributors in two respects: I am a judge as well as an academic; and I believe more deeply than other judges and academics, in either country, that the social sciences in general and economics in particular should inform both the study and the administration of the law.

Lecture One makes two linked arguments. First, through a comparison of two prominent writers on jurisprudence in the second half of this century, one English (H. L. A. Hart) and one American (Ronald Dworkin), I argue that trying to define 'law' is futile, distracting, and illustrative of the impoverishment of traditional legal theory. Second, I argue that the English legal system is closer in an important sense to the Continental legal system than it is to the American. The common language, the origins of the American legal system in the English, and the many superficial differences between the English and Continental systems and the equally many superficial similarities between the English and American systems have obscured this point—obscured, for example, the extent to which English

---

[1] P. S. Atiyah and Robert S. Summers, *Form and Substance in Anglo-American Law: A Comparative Study of Legal Reasoning, Legal Theory, and Legal Institutions* (1987). Another fine illustration of the genre is Maimon Schwarzschild, 'Class, National Character, and the Bar Reforms in Britain: Will There Always Be an England?' 9 *Connecticut Journal of International Law* 185 (1994). By 'English legal system' I mean the legal system of England and Wales, since Northern Ireland and especially Scotland have distinct legal systems.

barristers, when viewed functionally rather than nominally, are more properly regarded as judicial adjuncts than as advocates and, so regarded, alter the ratio between judges and lawyers in the direction of the Continental systems. The link to the first argument is what I claim is the Continental spirit of Hart's concept of law, which is in sharp contrast to the American spirit of Dworkin's. These eminent theorists mistake a local social phenomenon for a universal one. Functionally, England has a career judiciary, like the other European states, and the United States does not. Hart's concept of law describes how judges in a career judiciary think about law.

In Lecture Two I examine a number of English cases drawn primarily from the two fields in which English and American law overlap most completely—torts and contracts. I argue that while in general English judges use their common sense effectively to approximate the results that an economic analyst would recommend, they would do even better if they were more receptive to the economic approach to the common law—if they were, in this respect, a little more like American judges.

Lecture Three examines the differences between the English and American legal systems at the operational level as distinct from the jurisprudential and doctrinal levels, seeks to explain the differences, and warns against piecemeal reform of either system. The most striking difference is that the English legal system is much smaller than the American. The proximate causes are institutional. They include such things as the lower benefit-cost ratio of suit in England than in the United States, the near absence of contingent fees, and the greater simplicity and predictability of English law. The ultimate cause, however, may be that England has better alternatives to litigation as a means of social control than the United States does and so has not found it necessary to adopt measures, inevitably very costly, that facilitate the bringing of lawsuits. I conclude Lecture Three with some tentative suggestions, based on English experience, for the reform of American procedure, in particular the limiting of contingent fees. The English can learn something from Americans about the use of social science in judicial decisions; Americans can learn something from the English about how to limit the growth of litigation.

I have set forth in Appendix A an organization chart of the

English judiciary together with the official descriptions of the duties of circuit and district judges. The break between these two levels of judicial officers figures importantly in Lecture One, while the organization chart is necessary for an understanding of the intricate organization of the English legal system by those who are not part of the system. Appendix B describes an actual English appeal and may help the reader grasp the concrete differences between the English and American legal systems.

The analytic styles of the three lectures are different. The first is primarily jurisprudential, though it has (in its second half) a good deal of the sociological flavor of the third. The second lecture emphasizes the economic analysis of doctrine. The third is a mainly quantitative or systems comparison of the two legal systems, although I also touch on differences in 'national character'. My hope is that this three-cornered approach offers some fresh insights into an old subject—even that it may encourage similar comparisons with other legal systems—but of course these things are for the reader to decide. At the very least, some of my previously unpublished data, particularly in Lecture Three, may assist future comparativists, while the discussion of judicial administration in that and Lecture One, of jurisprudence in Lecture One, and of the common law in Lecture Two may have an interest for some readers that is independent of cross-national comparisons.

As is obvious from its brevity, the book only scratches the surface of its subject. I particularly regret not having had time to extend the comparison to the legal systems of the other English-speaking nations, and in particular Australia and Canada, which are intermediate in a number of interesting ways between the English and American systems.

Life has the disconcerting habit of not standing still for scholarly reflection. The English legal system, under financial and caseload pressures, as well as pressures exerted by the United Kingdom's accession to the European Union,[2] is under-going rapid change. I mention aspects of this change at various points in the book. But I must caution the reader that some of the contrasts I draw are based on traditional features of the

---

[2] See, for example, Jonathan E. Levitsky, 'The Europeanization of the British Legal Style' 42 *American Journal of Comparative Law* 347 (1994).

English system that may have eroded substantially by the time this book is published.

I have many acknowledgements. To the Oxford University Press, of course, for inviting me to give the lectures, and to Richard Hart and John Whelan, of the Press, for their wholly successful efforts to make the visit of my wife and myself to Oxford a pleasant and indeed memorable one. To Gareth Jones, for arranging for me to meet with leading members of the judiciary during my trip to England. To Lord Nicholas Browne-Wilkinson of the Appellate Committee of the House of Lords, to Sir Thomas Bingham, the Master of the Rolls, and to Lord Justice Christopher Staughton, for their generous assistance to my project. To Mr. Mark Camley of the Court Service, for leading me through the intricacies of English judicial statistics and for furnishing me with unpublished data and reports. To Lord David Windlesham and Professor Peter Birks for their gracious hospitality during our visit to Oxford. To Dr. John Gardner and Professors A. M. Honoré and Guenter Treitel for very helpful discussions of the subject matter of my lectures. To participants at seminars at Oxford and the University of Chicago Law School for helpful comments. To Kevin Cremin, Anup Malani, and Andrew Trask for excellent research assistance. And to Michael Boudin, Scott Brewer, Ruth Chang, David Cohen, David Currie, Neil Duxbury, Ronald Dworkin, Richard Epstein, William Eskridge, Elizabeth Garrett, Stephen Gilles, Thomas Grey, Gareth Jones, Daniel Klerman, Kevin Kordana, William Landes, Lawrence Lessig, Bernard Meltzer, Martha Nussbaum, Eric Posner, Todd Rakoff, Mark Ramseyer, Carolyn Shapiro, A. W. Brian Simpson, David Strauss, Cass Sunstein, and Alan Sykes for their exceedingly helpful comments on early drafts of the lectures.

Contents

Lecture One: Hart versus Dworkin, Europe versus America

If someone said to you, 'Time is an incredibly important and fundamental feature of the universe and human life, and therefore it is very important that we define it', you would be nonplussed. Time is very important, fundamental, the pervasive medium of action, and so on. But only the sort of person who wants to square the circle supposes that it either can be or needs to be defined. As St. Augustine put it, we know perfectly well what 'time' means—until we try to define it.

I react the same way to efforts to define 'law'. When I was a student at the Harvard Law School in its halcyon days, never did a professor ask the students in a class that I was in to define 'law'. There was a course in jurisprudence, where the question must have been raised, but relatively few students took the course and I was not one of them. When I teach jurisprudence I ask the students at the outset of the course to define 'law', and the definitions they offer are easily shown to be completely inadequate. But just as with 'time', though unable to define 'law' the students have no trouble using the word correctly, any more than I did before I became reflective in these matters, any more than other judges, and practicing lawyers, do.

In some settings it is feasible and even necessary to define 'law', for example, as we shall shortly see, where the word appears in a statute. Or if the question is, how many law courses should a law student be required to take in order to graduate, the word 'law' in the term 'law courses' is readily definable. What these examples have in common is that they concern the meaning of the word 'law' in a specific context or use. The question 'What is law?'. when posed in a class in jurisprudence or in a book or article on jurisprudence is, in contrast, acontextual.

A. *The Futility Thesis*

Because 'law' is so difficult, maybe impossible, to define acontextually, one might have expected Professor Hart to begin his famous book[1] by explaining why he thought it worthwhile to try to do so. Maybe he thought it necessary because he was writing a textbook for a course in jurisprudence, a course that to members of the 'analytic' school of jurisprudence, like Hart, is centrally though not solely concerned with the question, 'What is law?'[2] Or, given his philosophical milieu, he may have thought it obvious that the careful definition of concepts was an important task for philosophers. Professor A. M. Honoré has suggested to me that Hart may have thought it politically important to insist upon the distinction between law, morality, and brute force, since the merger of the three was one of the means by which Hitler had subverted traditional norms of legality in Germany.

Maybe Hart simply was content with the answer he had offered in an earlier work. But I get nothing out of that answer: 'The common mode of definition [of "law"] is ill adapted to the law and has complicated its exposition; its use has, I think, led at certain points to a divorce between jurisprudence and the study of the law at work, and has helped to create the impression that there are certain fundamental concepts that the lawyer cannot hope to elucidate without entering a forbidding jungle of

---

[1] H. L. A. Hart, *The Concept of Law* (2d ed. 1994). The first edition was published in 1961. The second edition, published posthumously, is unchanged except for Hart's 'Postscript'. As I shall be focusing on the postscript, the second edition is more usable for my purposes.

[2] See Joseph Raz, *The Concept of a Legal System: An Introduction to the Theory of Legal System* 1–2 (2d ed. 1980). I do not wish to be understood as anathematizing analytic jurisprudence, which I take to mean, nowadays at least, the application of the methods of analytic philosophy to law. See, for a notable example, H. L. A. Hart and Tony Honoré, *Causation in the Law* (2d ed. 1985). It is only the part of analytic jurisprudence (but it is a big part) that concerns itself with the question 'What is law?' that I argue is a cul-de-sac.

philosophical argument.'[3] Hart does not explain why jurisprudence should be married to the study of the law at work,
why lawyers should be concerned with elucidating fundamental
concepts, and why jurisprudence should be studied at all. The
answers to these questions are not self-evident, and later I shall
give a reason for applauding the divorce that Hart deplored.

I grant that even if the *word* 'law' cannot be defined, the
concept of law can be discussed; and that is after all Hart's title,
though he uses the word 'definition' a lot.[4] Philosophical
reflection on the concept of justice has been a fruitful enterprise
since Plato; for that matter, there is a philosophical literature on
time. I have nothing against philosophical speculation. But one
would like it to have some pay-off; *something* ought to turn on
the answer to the question 'What is law?' if the question is to be
worth asking by people who could use their time in other
socially valuable ways. Nothing does turn on it. I go further: the
central task of analytic jurisprudence is, or at least ought to be,
not to answer the question 'What is law?' but to show that it
should not be asked, because it only confuses matters.

Some might question this pragmatic view of philosophy—
might call it philistine—might say that philosophy like mathe-
matics has a beauty that is worth cultivating even if it has no
consequences for action. But that is not a characteristic retort of
professors of jurisprudence. They believe that their attempts to
elucidate the concept of law have implications for action. We
just saw that Hart regretted the divorce between the study of
jurisprudence and the study of the working level of the law. I do
not regret it.

I shall defend my skeptical position concerning the value of
asking 'What is law?' by examining three areas in which the
question has seemed to have a practical pay-off. Even if I am
right about all three, it will not *prove* my contention; to think it
will would be to commit the fallacy of induction, and upon a
very small sample. But if my examples are convincing they will

---

[3] 'Definition and Theory in Jurisprudence' in H. L. A. Hart, *Essays in
Jurisprudence and Philosophy* 21 (1983) (essay first published in 1953).
[4] Dworkin insists that Hart is trying to define law, that Hart's is, thus, a
semantic theory of law. Ronald Dworkin, *Law's Empire* 31–44 (1986).

at least challenge the conventional jurisprudential thinker to offer counterexamples.

Nuremberg

The British government wanted the Nazi leaders shot without a trial.[5] The Americans, however, wanted a trial, so a trial there was. One might be tempted to think that the difference between these positions was a difference over the meaning of 'law' and was in fact just the difference between the meanings ascribed to the word by Hart and (as we shall see) by Dworkin. If the principles enforced by the Nuremberg Tribunal were not 'law', there was no justification for holding a trial to determine whether the Nazi leaders had behaved illegally in enforcing their domestic laws. If those principles were law, and law that was supreme over domestic law in the same way that constitutional law in the United States trumps statutory law (or perhaps because the domestic law in question, being evil, was not 'really' law—an issue that cropped up in some postwar German cases as well), there was justification for holding a trial.

I doubt that the people at the highest decision-making level in the allied governments cared much about the conformity of the trials to a philosophically respectable concept of law. They should not have cared much. One thing they should have cared about and did care about was how best to stamp out Nazism for all time; and the Americans were correct, having in mind the psychology and traditions of the German people, that a public trial in which a full documentary record of the German atrocities would be created and subjected to the refining fires of adversarial procedure would be more effective than summary

---

[5] See the minutes of the War Cabinet of 12 April 1945. W.M. (45), 43d Conclusions, Minute 1, pp. 262–264 (Cab. 65/50); also Telford Taylor, *The Anatomy of the Nuremberg Trials: A Personal Memoir* 29–33 (1992); Ann Tusa and John Tusa, *The Nuremberg Trial* 61–67 (1984); Matthew Lippman, 'Nuremberg: Forty Five Years Later' 7 *Connecticut Journal of International Law* 1, 20–21 (1991); Lawrence Douglas, 'Film as Witness: Screening *Nazi Concentration Camps* before the Nuremberg Tribunal' 105 *Yale Law Journal* 449, 457–459 (1995). The British did want trials for lesser Nazis. Taylor, above, at 31. The difference between the British and American positions may have reflected a difference in political cultures. The British are accustomed to thinking of national leaders as being to some extent outside the law, since the Queen (or King) is, technically at least, the sovereign, and hence above the law. The United States has no sovereign.

executions in preventing a Nazi phoenix rising from the ashes. It would have been wrong to have been deflected from this course by an academic argument that the principles under which the Nazi leaders were to be tried were not 'law'. 'Trial' and 'law' are not even coterminous. Trials are a method of inquiry and (often) of exhibition or demonstration, and can be and sometimes are used when there is no actual legal dispute, as in the recent mock trial, before a panel of *three* U.S. Supreme Court Justices, to decide whether the Earl of Oxford was the real author of Shakespeare's plays.[6]

Just as 'trial' can be severed from law, so 'retroactive law', 'unenacted law', 'international law', and 'natural law' are not oxymorons, and all were available to give the Nuremberg trials a sufficient patina of legality to enable the trials to perform their educative and reformative role. Perhaps more than a patina. There are respectable arguments that even the unconventional charges against the Nazi leaders, such as waging aggressive war and committing crimes against humanity, had valid foundations in international law that was binding on Germany even during Hitler's rule.[7] I merely think that the conformity of the proceedings at Nuremberg to the best concept of 'law' was rightly not a central concern of those who had to decide whether to convene a war crimes trial.

Although I have emphasized as a goal of the Nuremberg trials the stamping out of Nazism in Germany, my argument would not be affected if other goals were assigned an equal or greater priority, such as the moral goal of giving the Nazi leaders a chance to defend themselves, or the goal of establishing a foundation for the punishment of war crimes committed in future wars, or (related to the last) the goal of bringing the rule of law to bear on relations among nations. All may be

[6] Irvin Molotsky, 'You-Know-Who Wrote the Plays, Judges Say' *New York Times*, 26 Sept. 1987, p. 1; Amy E. Schwartz, 'Three Justices, a Poetry-Starved Crowd and Shakespeare' *Washington Post*, 14 Oct. 1987, p. A19. Granted this was not a trial that resulted in the imposition of a sanction.

[7] See, for example, Bernard D. Meltzer, 'A Note on Some Aspects of the Nuremberg Debate' 14 *University of Chicago Law Review* 455 (1947); Quincy Wright, 'Legal Positivism and the Nuremberg Judgment' 42 *American Journal of International Law* 405 (1948); Stanley L. Paulson, 'Classical Legal Positivism at Nuremberg' 4 *Philosophy and Public Affairs* 132 (1975); Taylor, note 5 above, at 50–51.

worthwhile goals. But whether they are or not and how the trials might have contributed to their achievement are not issues illuminated by jurisprudential debate over the concept of law.

Some might even think that a greater value than any that I have mentioned would be to vindicate the rule of law in precisely the sense of 'law' that would later be proposed by Hart, and that therefore the trials were a mistake. You might think it a more important value in terms of long-run consequences, in which event we would have a practical political or sociological issue to debate, or a dictate of morality, which would translate the debate to another level, one that I am not prepared to follow you to. But in neither event would the debate be advanced by trying to answer the question 'What is law?'.

That some of the defendants were acquitted does not show that the Nuremberg trials were 'lawful' in a sense that might satisfy a Hart or even that the organizers of the trials cared about the issue. Had the judges not taken seriously the *forms* of law, including the principle that a judgment of guilt must be based on reliable and convincing evidence, the political objectives of proceeding against the Nazi leaders, as well as the additional moral or political goals that I have mentioned, would have been compromised.

Hart argued that unless legal and moral justice are held firmly apart in the mind of the community, the only mode of denunciation of evil laws is to call them no law, an artificial and unconvincing usage.[8] If Hart's prescription were followed, however, the Nuremberg trials would be open to the charge that the defendants were punished for obeying the law, whereas if positive law is deemed subordinate to natural law, just as American statutes are subordinate to the provisions of the U.S. Constitution, the charge fails. The latter, or antipositivist, approach seems to me the more effective rhetorically—for the alternative is to argue, very unattractively I should think, that *because* the Nazis could not be punished *legally* for obeying German law, they should be shot out of hand, or perhaps let off scot-free. But I do not think that more than rhetoric is at stake.

---

[8] H. L. A. Hart, 'Positivism and the Separation of Law and Morals' 71 *Harvard Law Review* 593 (1958). As far as I know, Hart never discussed the implications of his concept of law for the legality of the Nuremberg trials.

Prospective Overruling

Courts will sometimes overrule one of their decisions prospect-ively. That is, the new rule announced by the court will be applied only to lawsuits begun after the announcement. The implication is that the court is making new law, which could not have been anticipated, rather than rejecting the overruled precedent because the precedent violated (rather than declaring or establishing) existing law; that, in short, the court is acting like a legislature, making law rather than doing law. Hart's foremost follower, Joseph Raz, is explicit that whenever a judicial decision does not follow directly from a statute, from another judicial decision, or from custom (for Raz the three sources of law), the decision is making rather than applying law: prior to the decision there was *no law* on the issue decided.[9] In deciding a case in which the outcome is not dictated by one of the sources of law, judges necessarily are making moral choices, and morality is not a source of law in the positivist view.[10] The idea that legislation should be prospective is central to the concept of the rule of law, and thus to the criticism of the 'law' applied by the Nuremberg Tribunal. So, the argument continues, a case in which prospective overruling would be appropriate because the court was changing the law would necessarily be a case in which the court was stepping out of its judicial role and becoming a legislature, making rather than applying law. Lord Devlin deplored prospective overruling because 'it crosses the Rubicon that divides the judicial and the legislative powers. It turns judges into undisguised legislators.'[11]

But the jurisprudential debate over the propriety of prospect-ive overruling is easily bypassed by asking a practical question: Should the community's reliance on a previous decision be a weight in the balance when the court is considering whether to overrule that decision, or should reliance be removed as a factor

[9] 'The Inner Logic of the Law' in Raz, *Ethics in the Public Domain: Essays in the Morality of Law and Politics* 222, 232 (1994).

[10] Id. at 232–233.

[11] Patrick Devlin, *The Judge* 12 (1979). Devlin was a distinguished member of the Appellate Committee of the House of Lords; one of his influential judicial opinions figures prominently in Lecture Two.

by authorizing courts to overrule decisions prospectively? The argument for authorizing prospective overruling is that otherwise the courts will be unduly hampered in reexamining old decisions. The argument against is that it will make them too quick to overrule their previous decisions. Resolution of the debate requires striking a balance between the values of continuity and of creativity in the judicial process, a difficult task but one that, being practical, is not illuminated by asking, 'What is law?'. If we decide that prospective overruling destabilizes the law unduly, we can say that Hart and Raz and Devlin must be right—when judges overrule precedents they are creating rather than applying law. But what would be the utility of this further step?

The Rules of Decision Act

The issue in the famous American cases of *Swift* v. *Tyson*[12] and *Erie R.R.* v. *Tompkins*[13] was whether the 'laws' of the various U.S. states should be understood to include the common law of the states or just their statutes. If the broader understanding was correct, as held in *Erie*, overruling *Swift*, then, under the statute that prescribes the rules of decision in cases that are in federal court solely because of the diverse citizenship of the parties and not because the suit is based on federal law,[14] federal courts should apply state common law, as well as state statutes, in such cases. If the narrower understanding was correct, as the Supreme Court had thought in *Swift*, federal courts should apply general common law not tethered to the decisional law of any particular state. The choice between these positions has been thought to be a choice between different concepts of law. Thus Professor Lessig argues that when 'the notion that the common law is found, not made . . . changed . . . this *forced* a reallocation of institutional responsibility (from federal courts to state courts). The old view [that of *Swift*] depended upon this earlier understanding of the common law; when this understanding changed, so, too, did institutional allocations *have* to

---

[12] 41 U.S. (16 Pet.) 1 (1842). The holding in *Swift* was actually merely declaratory of what was already the settled practice of the federal courts.
[13] 304 U.S. 64 (1938).
[14] Rules of Decision Act, now 28 U.S.C. §1652.

change'.[15] Holmes had famously argued against the narrow understanding on the ground that all law emanates from a sovereign, and so when state courts create common law they are doing it as delegates of the state legislature, just as if they were passing a statute.[16] They are not, as *Swift* had assumed, taking a stab at discovering the applicable principles of 'the' common law in the sense of a body of principles that is not the emanation of any identifiable sovereign, that is instead a composite of the decisional law of many different sovereigns plus principles that might be invented by federal judges in the very course of deciding a diversity case.

Had the judges in *Swift* and the other cases in its line believed that common law *could not* be thought of as being 'law' in the same sense as statute law, they would have been making a mistake. It would have been a mistake caused by taking seriously the question 'What is law?'—and so an argument for that very divorce between jurisprudence and practical law that Hart deplored, and more broadly for the view that the proper office of philosophy is to dispel philosophy, or at least conceptualism.[17] But if the judges in the *Swift* line believed that Congress had not intended 'laws' to include common law (or that their intentions were inscrutable or irrelevant) and were untroubled by the constitutional argument later made by Justice Brandeis in *Erie* that Article III of the U.S. Constitution does not authorize federal judges to create state rules of decision, or if they thought that it would be better on the whole if federal judges tried to create a uniform common law for use in diversity cases, then Holmes's argument would have fallen flat. For the issue would then have been either (or both) the 'legalistic' one of the intent behind the Rules of Decision Act (and Article III), or

[15] Lawrence Lessig, 'The Limits of Lieber' 16 *Cardozo Law Review* 2249, 2266 n. 57 (1995) (emphasis added).

[16] See *Black & White Taxicab & Transfer Co.* v. *Brown & Yellow Taxicab & Transfer Co.*, 276 U.S. 518, 533 (1928) (Holmes, J. dissenting).

[17] Compare John Ellis's antidefinition of 'literature'. He shows, very much in the spirit of the later Wittgenstein, that there is no set of properties that mark off literary from other writings (just as, I would add, there is no set of properties that marks off law from other social practices). Literature is simply the set of writings that happens, for a variety of reasons, to be used in a context remote from the one in which they were created. John M. Ellis, *The Theory of Literary Criticism: A Logical Analysis* (1974).

the practical one of trading off the added incentive to forum-shopping and added uncertainty of legal obligation created by *Swift's* approach against the pressure which that approach exerts for greater nationwide uniformity and integration of law. To either way of framing the issue, the question 'What is law?' makes no contribution. All that Holmes did was to use one inadequate definition of law to knock down another.

The jurisprudential debate in *Swift* and *Erie* illustrates the difference between contextual and acontextual definitions of 'law'. In so far as the issue in those cases turned on the interpretation of the rules of decision statute, the judges had to grapple with the question what is 'law' (or 'laws')—as the term is used in the statute—just as judges have to do by virtue of the provision of the Administrative Procedure Act that forbids a reviewing court to invalidate agency action when there is no law to apply, the matter having been committed to the agency's discretion.[18] These are questions within the professional competence of lawyers. They have nothing to do with philosophy. The acontextual question 'What is law?' has only to do with philosophy.

B. *So Why Is the Question Asked?*

Although I do not think that the question 'What is law?' in the universalistic sense in which the question is posed in jurisprudence ever has to be asked or answered, this leaves unexplained *why* it is asked. There must be *something* at stake for people of the caliber of Hart and Dworkin to spend so much time worrying it. I think the answer, or at least part of it, is that 'law' sounds better than 'politics' to most people. So if you want the judges to keep a low profile—play a modest role in the formation of public policy—you define 'law' narrowly and if you want them to throw their weight around in the policy arena you define 'law' broadly. This is the basic difference between legal positivists, such as Holmes and Hart (and perhaps Bickel and Bork)[19] on the one hand, and Dworkin, Lon Fuller, and other antipositivists on the other.

---

[18] 5 U.S.C. §701(a)(2); see *Heckler* v. *Chaney*, 470 U.S. 821, 830 (1985).

[19] As argued in Anthony J. Sebok, 'Misunderstanding Positivism' 93 *Michigan Law Review* 2054, 2058, 2126–2132 (1995).

I do not mean to suggest that judicial modesty is *entailed* by positivism.[20] Positivism is a concept of law, not a concept of what judges should do. A positivist might think it perfectly all right for judges to legislate, at least within the bounds fixed by the nature of the judicial office and the relation of the judiciary to the other branches of government. This seems, indeed, to have been Holmes's view. But today—especially in the United States—few judges or other legal professionals are comfortable with such a stance. The legislative process is in rather bad odor today because of increased recognition of the role of ignorance, fraud, and the 'special interests' in it, so that judges do not want to be confused with legislators. And the activism of the Supreme Court and the other federal (and some state) courts during the 1960s and 1970s is now widely regarded as having gone 'too far'. America is in a period of judicial retrenchment.

I go further. The tendency today is for the positivist to be, not a pragmatist like Holmes, but a formalist (which Holmes was only occasionally, mainly in cases dealing with contracts or with sovereign immunity). Again, positivism does not entail formalism.[21] But they are a comfortable couple, so one is not surprised to find that English judges are at once more positivistic and more formalistic than their American counterparts. A formalist hews to deduction as the model of judicial reasoning, and deduction merely brings to light what is contained in the premises; it does not add to them. Hence deduction from the authorized sources of law, by adding nothing to the sources, ensures the lawfulness of the decision so obtained. The judge who uses deduction to generate his decisions is doing law, not straying outside it, perhaps into politics.

The motives for wanting to keep judges out of politics are various. In Holmes's case it may have been both the intellectual's natural fastidiousness about politics and a desire (influenced by the growing prestige of science in his formative years and the fact that his father was a distinguished medical scientist) to think that what he was doing as a lawyer and judge was science,

---

[20] Cf. Sebok, note 19 above.

[21] Joseph Raz, 'On the Autonomy of Legal Reasoning' in *Ethics in the Public Domain*, note 9 above, at 310, 314–319; see also Richard A. Posner, *The Problems of Jurisprudence* 10–11 (1990).

for science is not (despite what some English sociologists of science say!) a branch of politics. In the case of Hart and of the English judiciary traditionally, the high incomes, cosy clubbiness, and high prestige of the judges are seen as a fair trade for the judges keeping their noses out of the political arena.[22] 'As the courts had come to have less concern with modern problems, and as the judges articulated for themselves a position which seemed to make their predispositions irrelevant, there was a corresponding increase in the respect in which the judges were held.'[23]

I do not suggest that Hart himself was motivated by admiration for the caste character of the English judiciary. Quite the contrary. He was, as I understand it, a life-long socialist. Probably he disliked the political views of English judges and wanted so far as possible to keep those views from influencing adjudication and through it public policy.[24] His position resembles that of the early twentieth-century liberals in the United States who opposed the efforts of conservative judges to imbue the Constitution with natural law principles such as liberty of contract. Holmes, a positivist, was the leader of the opposition. Dworkin, in contrast, applauds the efforts of liberal Supreme Court Justices to do just that with the natural law principles of which Dworkin approves, and so he plumps for a definition of law broad enough to encompass even what most other admirers of Chief Justice Warren would acknowledge was political judging. For Devlin, in this respect a positivist ally of Hart (though they disagreed on other matters), the U.S. Supreme Court is not a court at all, but 'an organ of government . . . In three fields—racial desegregation, voting rights, and reform of criminal procedure—it has legislated where consensus was non-existent or at least doubtful.'[25] The list could be considerably lengthened. As the passage I just quoted implies, Devlin permits judges to 'legislate' when they have a consensus behind

---

[22] This is very much the flavor of Devlin's book. See note 11 above.

[23] Brian Abel-Smith and Robert Stevens, *Lawyers and the Courts: A Sociological Study of the English Legal System 1750–1965* 125 (1967).

[24] As they had done in the nineteenth century, obstructing social legislation, id., ch. 4; Devlin, note 11 above, at 15, and as the German judiciary did under Hitler by interpreting Nazi legislation expansively. Richard A. Posner, *Overcoming Law* 155–156 (1995).   [25] Devlin, note 11 above, at 7.

them—that is, when no significant segment of the public would question the wisdom of what they are doing. He gives the example of abrogating the wonderfully quaint common law rule that forbade a landlord to collect rent from a tenant couple whom the landlord knew to be unmarried. He makes plain his disagreement with rigid adherence to stare decisis. But the abrogation of the rent rule would still be legislating, in his view, rather than doing law.[26]

I do not accuse Hart or Dworkin of tendentiousness. But it is a fact that theories of law generally coincide with the theorist's political preferences.

C. Hart's Postscript

I want to elaborate these views with the help of the fascinating postscript that Hart wrote to *The Concept of Law*, in which he examines Dworkin's criticism of the book.[27] Hart is on inherently weak ground, since he is defending the indefensible—an acontextual definition of 'law'. Were the shoe on the other foot and Dworkin trying to respond to his critics, he would be on equally weak ground, which I think is where you will find him if you read his sometimes rather sour answers to his critics.[28]

The basic concept of law that Hart sets forth in his book is well known. Law is a system of rules. One of these (illustrative of the 'secondary' rules that are necessary to the effectuation of the 'primary' rules, the rules of legal obligation themselves) is a rule of recognition that enables people to know when a particular rule is part of the system of legal rules rather than part of some other system. The rules are applied by judges, who correspond to umpires in games, another rule-based activity. If umpires had discretion whether or not to enforce the rules, games would fall apart. Similarly, if 'scorer's discretion' were allowed to judges, the legal system would fall apart. Legal rules, however, are often less precise than rules of games (they have what Hart calls

---

[26] See id. at 13.

[27] 'Postscript' in Hart, note 1 above, at 238.

[28] See, for example, Ronald Dworkin, 'Pragmatism, Right Answers, and True Banality' in *Pragmatism in Law and Society* 359 (Michael Brint and William Weaver eds. 1991).

'open texture') and therefore judges sometimes have to decide cases other than by applying a rule. In these cases, which Hart in the postscript calls 'legally unregulated',[29] the judges exercise discretion and in fact are legislators—makers of rules. As *unelected* legislators they are bound to proceed modestly if they conceive their 'creative' decisions as being legislative. If instead, as Dworkin believes, judges are doing, not making, law when they decide contestable issues, they are acting within the scope of their authorized function and professional competence and need not be so timid.

It is striking that neither the first nor the second edition of Hart's book contains an index reference to 'common law'. Dworkin, in contrast, rarely discusses legal doctrines other than common law doctrines or doctrines that the Supreme Court has excogitated out of the vaguest provisions of the U.S. Constitution, provisions that judges have treated as essentially directives to the courts to create constitutional doctrine by the common law method. The common law is an embarrassment to Hart's account.[30] In the postscript, while acknowledging that 'in some systems of law, as in the United States, the ultimate criteria of legal validity might explicitly incorporate besides pedigree, principles of justice or substantive moral values, and these may form the content of legal constitutional restraints',[31] he is still saying nothing about the common law, though it is a part of English as well as of American law, indeed a bigger part. It is difficult to fit the common law to the idea, which is fundamental to Hart's positivism, of a rule of recognition, because the materials out of which judges make common law are not limited to enactments of positive law. It is no answer, as Holmes thought, to conceive of the common law as just a body of legislation promulgated by judges as the delegates of legislatures. That would mean that any time in the course of deciding a common law case the judges modified, extended, or even just refined a rule of the common law—and of course these are the sorts of things that judges in common law countries are doing all

---

[29] Hart, note 1 above, at 252.
[30] A. W. B. Simpson, 'The Common Law and Legal Theory' in *Oxford Essays in Jurisprudence: Second Series* 77, 80–84 (A. W. B. Simpson ed. 1973).
[31] Hart, note 1 above, at 247.

the time, even in a system such as the English that lays great emphasis on the desirability of judges standing by previous decisions—they would not be judging; they would be legislating. This view, which is indeed that of Raz and Devlin,[32] not only overlooks important differences between common law judges on the one hand and legislatures on the other; it also implies the startling proposition that *most* of what American appellate judges do, other than when deciding appeals that involve purely factual issues or are so open and shut that they can be decided without an opinion, is legislation, not adjudication. A further objection to the positivist conception is that judges and lawyers are not aware of a division between the judge as applier and as maker of law. There is no point in the process of argument or decision at which the judges or lawyers say, 'We've exhausted the law; it's time to legislate.'.

I am being a little unfair in picking on Hart. The judicial process is not the focus of his book. He was more interested in redefining legal positivism, which to Austin, Bentham, and Holmes (as we glimpsed in discussing the *Swift–Erie* debate) had meant that law was not law unless it emanated from some sovereign. Hart replaced this idea with that of secondary rules, in particular the rule of recognition. But he could not avoid discussing the judicial process, since it is a testing ground for any answer to 'What is law?'. By discussing the judicial process without reconciling the practice of judges to his theory of positivism, he opened himself to Dworkin's criticisms.

Dworkin is right to stress the differences between judges and real legislators, although the differences are smaller in the United States than in England. Parliament has taken upon itself more responsibility vis-à-vis the courts for making the rules of law than American legislatures have vis-à-vis American courts.[33] If some doctrine of English law needs patching up, the English judge can decide, with a better conscience than his American

[32] See text at notes 9 and 10 above; Devlin, note 11 above, ch. 1.
[33] See Patrick S. Atiyah, 'Judicial–Legislative Relations in England' in *Judges and Legislators: Toward Institutional Comity* 129 (Robert A. Katzmann ed. 1988); William S. Jordan, III, 'Legislative History and Statutory Interpretation: The Relevance of English Practice' 29 *University of San Francisco Law Review* 1 (1994).

counterpart could do, to leave the matter to the legislature to correct.[34]

Dworkin lays particular stress on how judges differ from legislators with regard to what judges properly can consider when they are in their rulemaking mode—only principles, he argues, whereas legislators may also consider policies.[35] Dworkin makes this distinction so that no one will suppose that judges are merely legislators in robes. I think he exaggerates the difference between legislative and judicial rulemakers. It is true that judges are supposed to be, and the conditions of their employment as well as the decision-making procedures and methods that they use encourage them to be, more principled than legislatures, less swayed by narrow special interest groups and by ignorant public opinion. But what Dworkin calls 'policies' can be principled, and some of his principles strike some observers as highly debatable policies.[36] This is a detail. The important point is that if a big part of judging consists not of 'legislating' in Hart's sense of an essentially uncanalized exercise of discretion, but of the methodical application of principles and policies drawn from a world of thought and feeling not circumscribed by lawyers' knowledge, the idea of law as a system of rules is undermined. Hart replies that principles are a kind of rule—a weak or vague rule, like a presumption (illustrating a weak rule) or a standard, such as negligence (illustrating a vague or multifactored rule), or a 'latent' rule.[37] He misses Dworkin's point. Principles and rules are related hierarchically rather than coordinately. Rules mediate between principles and action. They translate principles into directives for action. They are subtended by principles. The

[34] A better conscience but not a perfect conscience. If the doctrine affects only a small number of people, Parliament may not get around to reforming it, because of the competing demands on its time. Christopher Staughton, 'The Role of the Law Commission: Parliamentary and Public Perceptions of Statute Law' 16 *Statute Law Review* 7, 9 (1995).

[35] For a compendious statement of his position to a British audience, see Ronald Dworkin, 'Political Judges and the Rule of Law' 64 *Proceedings of the British Academy* 259, 261 (1978).

[36] For a recent effort, within Dworkin's framework, to fix (other) bounds on what is admissible in the name of 'principle' to shape legal decision-making, see John Rawls, *Political Liberalism* 236 (1993).

[37] Hart, note 1 above, at 268.

judges make the rules out of principles but there is no rule of recognition telling them what principles to use in this constructive endeavor or even where to look for principles. In Raz's reformulation of legal positivism, principles are not law because their source (the common morality, the teaching of the great philosophers, or whatever) is not a source of law.[38]

Hart acknowledges that judges when they act as legislators are subject to limitations from which legislators are free. Apart from limitations of a purely *Realpolitik* character, the judge must 'act as a conscientious legislator would by deciding according to his own beliefs and values.'.[39] This is not much of a concession. To decide according to one's 'own beliefs and values' is not to decide in accordance with, or to be disciplined by, principle or policy. One is therefore not surprised to find Hart implying on the preceding page that whenever the judge decides an indeterminate case, that is, a case in which 'no decision either way is dictated by the law', he is 'step[ping] outside the law'.[40] In saying this Hart shows that he really does think that law is a system of rules.

Devlin, more interested than Hart in the judicial process, distinguishes between the rules of law and the justice of the case. He recognizes the tension between them, recognizes that judges sometimes 'stretch the law' to do substantive justice— and does not disapprove of this practice, provided the judges do not acknowledge that they are stretching the law.[41] Devlin cannot admit a place in the concept of law for the moral feelings that shape our response to the 'equities' of a legal dispute. When judges act on those feelings they are behaving lawlessly and so they must conceal what they are doing. This is a Leo Strauss or (Dostoevsky's) Grand Inquisitor conception of the judge. In contrast, Dworkin deems the judge's moral feelings,

---

[38] See, for example, 'The Problem about the Nature of Law' in Raz, note 9 above, at 179.

[39] Hart, note 1 above, at 273. One might have thought that a legislator would have a representative function and therefore could not properly decide *only* according to his own beliefs and values.

[40] Id. at 272. Raz is explicit about this, as we have seen. See also 'Authority, Law, and Morality' in Raz, note 9 above, at 194, 213.

[41] Devlin, note 11 above, at 90–93.

when properly disciplined and reasoned, 'principles' and principles part of law, which is what most American judges would think.

In 'strong' versions of positivism, including Hart's, a necessary condition of making a rule of primary obligation a rule of law is that it be picked out by a legal system's rule of recognition. In 'weak' versions, it is a sufficient condition. For the first type of positivist all the Nazi laws were indeed law but the 'law' applied by the Nuremberg Tribunal was not, while for the second type of positivist, the 'weak', the Nazi laws were law but the law applied by the Tribunal also may have been law. A 'strong' natural lawyer insists that law is law only if it conforms to natural law. A 'weak' natural lawyer, however, is indistinguishable from a 'weak' positivist. This appears to be Dworkin's position. He does not deny that the Nazi laws were laws.[42] But he thinks that the natural law type declarations of the Supreme Court in the free-wheeling era of Earl Warren's Chief Justiceship were also law. Dworkin is not a natural lawyer in the traditional sense of one who believes that legal obligations can be derived from religous or other metaphysical principles. But he is emphatically not a positivist in Hart's strong sense, and he has not resisted the labeling of his theory of adjudication as a natural law theory.[43]

I do think that Hart is *descriptively* though not semantically more accurate in his account of judicial activity in the open area, the area where the rules run out. He is right to point out that the cases in this area are frequently indeterminate and that in deciding such cases the judge is making a value choice based on intuition and personal experience—albeit a choice less likely than a legislator's to reflect the pressure of special interest groups or the passions of the moment—rather than engaging solely in analysis, reflection, or some special mode of inquiry called 'legal reasoning'. But I disagree with his belief that the proper characterization of what the judges are doing when they do these things is 'stepping out of the law'. It depends on what

---

[42] Dworkin, note 4 above, at 102–108.
[43] See Ronald A. Dworkin, ' "Natural Law" Revisited' 34 *University of Florida Law Review* 165 (1982).

is expected of judges, and this differs across different legal systems. Likewise I think that Dworkin exaggerates the determinateness of legal reasoning and that it is no accident that the controversial decisions of the Supreme Court that he declares to be principled and lawful conform to his political preferences. What he should be saying is that when judges render political decisions they are still doing law, because law is interpenetrated with politics. One thing law is is simply the *activity* of judges, and that activity frequently has a political dimension.[44] Not that 'lawless judge' is an oxymoron. It means that the judge is being *too* political to conform to the reigning conception in the judge's society of the outer bounds of a judge's decisional freedom. But that is all it means.

Let me set issues of candor to one side. Where Dworkin's concept of law as embracing principles as well as rules falters is in its corollary, which he has not hesitated to draw, that a judge who conceives of his function more narrowly than Dworkin thinks he should and so declines to appeal to a broad range of principles in deciding new cases, or who appeals to what Dworkin considers mere policies rather than principles, is lawless.[45] This exercise in persuasive definition would strike most English judges as preposterous—should we conclude that English judges are lawless?

Yet if we move to a high enough level of abstraction, we find a significant area of agreement between Hart and Dworkin. For Hart, most of what appellate judges having a discretionary jurisdiction, such as the Supreme Court of the United States or the Appellate Commitee of the House of Lords, do is to legislate; for Dworkin, it is to practice applied moral philosophy. These sound very different but Raz explains that, whenever conscientious judges go beyond the application of rules (and that is very often, if they are appellate judges), they perforce engage in moral reasoning, for they are making normative decisions that do not originate in the law.[46]

---

[44] Posner, note 21 above, at 220–239.
[45] See, for example, Ronald Dworkin, 'The Bork Nomination' *New York Review of Books*, Aug. 13, 1987, p. 3, reprinted in 9 *Cardozo Law Review* 101 (1987).
[46] See note 9 above.

II. THE CONTINENTAL CHARACTER OF THE ENGLISH
LEGAL SYSTEM

The preface to *The Concept of Law* says that the reader is free to take the book as 'an essay in descriptive sociology'[47] and so taken, especially in contrast to Dworkin's writings, it is illuminating as a stylized description of the modern English legal system by a knowledgeable insider, just as Dworkin's jurisprudence is illuminating as a stylized description of the methods of liberal Supreme Court Justices, and just as the discussion of corrective justice in the *Nicomachean Ethics* is illuminating as a stylized description of the Athenian legal system of Aristotle's day. What is striking about Hart's book when it is regarded as description (or self-description) rather than as philosophy is that it is equally descriptive of the Continental as of the English legal system though not, as I hope I have persuaded you, of the American.

Hart's emphasis on law as rules, his lack of interest in the common law, his conception of the judge as primarily an applier of rules laid down by legislatures, and his desire to demarcate a realm that is law and not politics, add up to a mindset characteristic of Continental legal systems since the French Revolution but not of the English legal system before this century or of the American legal system at any point in its history.[48] When you look away from Hart's book and at actual institutions, this impression is reinforced rather than, as one would expect, contradicted. It is true that many of the differences, real or apparent, among the English, American, and Continental legal systems are favorable to grouping the English

---

[47] Hart, note 1 above, at v.

[48] Hart acknowledges the similarity of his concept of law to that of Hans Kelsen, the Austrian legal positivist, while noting a number of differences. E.g., id. at 292–295. And there is an evident similarity between the influential views of the late-nineteenth-century English lawyer A. V. Dicey and the concept of the *Rechtsstaat* that is so prominent a feature of Continental, especially German, legal thinking. Compare Dicey, *Introduction to the Study of the Law of the Constitution*, ch. 4 (4th ed. 1893), esp. pp. 191–192, with William Ewald, 'Comparative Jurisprudence (I): What Was It Like to Try a Rat?' 143 *University of Pennsylvania Law Review* 1889, 2053–2055 (1995).

system with the American. English judges have more prestige than American judges, who in turn have more prestige than Continental judges; a related point is that the ratio of judges to lawyers is lowest in England, next lowest in America, and highest on the Continent. The English system places greatest emphasis on 'orality', the Continental least, the American in the middle. The English legal system is the least 'bureaucratic', the Continental the most, the American again in the middle. The English and American systems are adversarial, the Continental inquisitorial. As Max Weber emphasized, English law is less completely rationalized than French or German law; there is less emphasis on 'theory', on conceptual order.

Some of these points are marginal, especially to appellate decision-making. This is true of the ratio of talk to paper, of the differences in trial procedure or doctrinal tidiness, and of prestige, which depends on relative salaries in different branches of the legal profession and the prestige of intellectual versus practical activities in the society at large. Others are misleading, such as the greater emphasis on theory in the Continental legal systems. The important difference in terms of substance rather than mere form, so far as receptivity to theory is concerned, and it is a difference between the United States and the rest of the world, concerns receptivity not to legal conceptualism but to social science, to which the Germans, for example, are as hostile as the English.[49] Other differences between the English and Continental legal systems are, as we are about to see, artifacts of a confusion, common in legal thought, of the nominal with the functional.

A. Barristers as Judicial Adjuncts

If the concept of 'judge' is reconceived in terms of the functions that different segments of a legal profession play, then the ratio of judges to lawyers is far higher in the English than in the American system, just as it is far higher in the Continental legal systems than in the American. It is true that only 651 judges in

---

[49] See Christian Kirchner, 'The Difficult Reception of Law and Economics in Germany' 11 *International Review of Law and Economics* 277 (1991), esp. 284–286.

England have a general jurisdiction.[50] The corresponding number in the United States today is slightly more than 10,000,[51] which is 15 times greater, yet there are not 15 times as many American as English lawyers but only a little more than 10 times as many. (There are about 800,000 American lawyers and about 70,000 English barristers and solicitors, of whom almost 8,000 are barristers.[52]) But in reality the barristers are more like junior judges than like lawyers as we think of lawyers in the United States, and when they are reclassified as judges the ratio of judges to lawyers changes dramatically in the direction of the Continental pattern.

The barristers depend entirely on the good will of the judges, who naturally insist that the barristers play a helping role in adjudication. The reasons for this dependence are several. One is simply that there are so few judges and barristers. The principal significance of the separation of barristers from solicitors, and specifically of the barristers' traditional monopoly of litigation in the higher courts (the High Court, the Court of Appeal, and the Appellate Committee of the House of Lords),[53] may lie in keeping the bar small. There are so few barristers and

[50] This is the number of judges (as of 1 April 1995) down to and including circuit judges; the district judges (formerly 'district registrars'), which are the next rung below, appear to correspond to American magistrates. The number 651 is computed from Lord Chancellor's Department's Court Service Annual Report 1994–95 14–15 (July 1995). See Appendix A at the end of this book for an organization chart of the English court system and descriptions of the duties of circuit and district judges.

[51] See my book The Federal Courts: Challenge and Reform, ch. 1 (2d ed., forthcoming from Harvard University Press in 1996). The total number of American judges is almost three times as great as the figure in the text, but by confining my count to judges having a 'general jurisdiction' I exclude a host of specialized lower-level judicial officers, mainly traffic and domestic-relations judges. The principal counterparts in England to these judicial officers are the magistrates, of which more anon.

[52] Editorial, 'A Good Recession' 144 New Law Journal 1613 (1994); Frederick Lawton, 'Crisis at the Bar—Why the Bar Must Urgently Consider the Future of Training and Practice' Law Society's Gazette no. 1, p. 9 (1994).

[53] See the organization chart in Appendix A. (The Privy Council, the fourth of the higher courts, is staffed by the members of the Appellate Committee of the House of Lords.) Solicitors are traditionally allowed to practice in the county courts and the Crown Court and before magistrates. The Courts and Legal Services Act 1990, 27–33, broke the barristers' monopoly, in principle anyway, of litigating cases in the higher courts. The long-run effects of the Act on the English legal system are not yet visible.

judges that a barrister is likely to appear repeatedly before the same judge, so if he fails to please him the first time his future will be clouded—all the more so as word will spread rapidly among so small a corps of judges. The barrister who arouses the enmity of a judge will be a pariah from the start. The virtual abolition of the civil jury in England reinforces the dependence of the barristers on the good will of the judges, as does the insulation between barrister and client. (The solicitor hires the barrister through the latter's clerk.) That insulation makes it difficult for a barrister to obtain clients by dazzling impressionable lay persons—a big problem in the United States, where incompetent lawyers, and known to be such both by judges and by other lawyers, often wow naïve clients.

The fact that judgeships are 'pensionable jobs to move into when they [that is, the barristers] are getting old'[54] is another source of the felt dependence of the bar on the good will of the judiciary. Being self-employed, barristers do not have secure pension expectations. I am told that formerly virtually every barrister in good standing could count on some sort of judicial appointment as he approached retirement. And the senior rank of barristers—Queen's Counsel (also known as silks)—are appointed to that rank by the Lord Chancellor, the head of the English judiciary, after consultation with the judges before whom the candidate for 'silk' appeared. Queen's Counsel are the highest-paid barristers.[55] This means that the judges control the livelihood of the bar to a degree that would be unthinkable in the United States. And traditionally only Queen's Counsel are eligible for appointment as judges of the higher courts. The significance of the barrister's promotion ladder for the vigor of advocacy is brought out in a passing remark by Professor Abel: 'some clients may prefer a junior [barrister] who has abandoned the hope of being appointed a silk or a judge *and thus may be a more vigorous advocate.'*.[56]

An important quasi-judicial role of barristers is refusing to

---

[54] *Jackson's Machinery of Justice* 353 (J. R. Spencer ed. 1989). For good descriptions of the English bar, see id., chs. 28 and 30; P. S. Atiyah and Robert S. Summers, *Form and Substance in Anglo-American Law: A Comparative Study of Legal Reasoning, Legal Theory, and Legal Institutions* 360–369 (1987).

[55] Richard L. Abel, *The Legal Profession in England and Wales* 122–123 (1988).

[56] Id. at 100 (emphasis added).

accept unmeritorious cases.[57] In effect, like judges they 'dismiss' these cases. Rare it is in the United States for a paying client to be unable to find a lawyer willing to file his case, even if the case is frivolous and even though there are sanctions for filing frivolous cases. American lawyers lack the incentives of British barristers to avoid annoying judges with marginal cases. Another reason for the greater forbearance of barristers is that the absence of contingent-fee contracts[58] removes the temptation to roll the dice by bringing a case that, while unlikely to succeed, will pay off handsomely if it does. A contingent fee, moreover, is a form of incentive compensation. The lawyer who takes a case on a contingent-fee basis has a greater stake in winning than the lawyer who is paid on a strict hourly basis, win or lose. The former will press harder for victory,[59] and by doing so may compromise his position as an 'officer of the court'.

Against this it should be noted that concern with reputation, an important factor in obtaining future business, will exert pressure on the hourly-fee lawyer to do his best. In addition, a contingent-fee contract may give the lawyer a greater incentive to decline a weak case than if he is paid on an hourly basis,[60] since the cost of losing is shifted from the client to the lawyer. 'May', not 'shall', because the lawyer may accept the weak case and just put less work into it, so that the expected profit to him from taking the case is still positive. And concern with reputation will operate on the contingent-fee lawyer as well as on the hourly-fee lawyer; if these inducements are assumed to

---

[57] Atiyah and Summers, note 54 above, at 368.

[58] This has been changed recently; lawyers may now make a contract with their client to receive a double fee if their client wins and nothing if the client loses. This is an example of piecemeal reform of the English legal system, which I discuss in the third lecture.

[59] H. Gravelle and M. Waterson, 'No Win, No Fee: Some Economics of Contingent Legal Fees' 103 *Economic Journal* 1205, 1207 (1993), and references cited there. This concern lies behind the traditional rule forbidding contingent fees in criminal cases. Peter Lushing, 'The Fall and Rise of the Criminal Contingent Fee' 82 *Journal of Criminal Law and Criminology* 498 (1991).

[60] Kevin M. Clermont and John D. Currivan, 'Improving on the Contingent Fee' 63 *Cornell Law Review* 529, 571–573 (1978); Thomas J. Miceli, 'Do Contingent Fees Promote Excessive Litigation?' 23 *Journal of Legal Studies* 211 (1994). For a comprehensive analysis of the complicated economics of contingent fees by an English economist, see Neil Rickman, 'The Economics of Contingency Fees in Personal Injury Litigation' 10 *Oxford Review of Economic Policy* 34 (1994).

be equal, then clearly the contingent-fee lawyer will have the greater incentive to fight hard for his client. The contingent-fee screen is inherently imperfect, moreover, because contingent-fee contracts are not mandatory. It is always open to the determined client to hire a lawyer on an hourly basis if the lawyer considers the prospects of victory too remote to justify his taking the case on a contingent basis.

Another feature of English but not American procedure, the 'loser pays' rule—the losing party must reimburse a substantial part of the winner's attorney's fees—facilitates the barrister's performance of his screening role by discouraging the marginal claimant from shopping for a complaisant barrister to handle his case. The loser-pays rule also reduces the friction between judges and lawyers that is produced by the American practice, erratic as it is, of sanctioning lawyers for bringing frivolous suits or interposing frivolous defenses. The American practice may be erratic *because* of the friction it produces.

Barristers perform de jure as well as de facto judicial roles.[61] The policy of the current Lord Chancellor is that 'before being considered for any judicial post, a candidate must have served in that or a similar post in a part-time capacity for long enough to establish his or her competence and suitability.'.[62] These part-time judges, called 'recorders', 'assistant recorders', and 'deputy High Court judges', accounted in 1994 for 17 percent of all judicial sitting days.[63] Just as in a career judiciary, English judges gain judicial experience by trying small cases before being entrusted with big ones. Thus, according to Atiyah and Summers, 'The English bar is almost an apprenticeship for becoming a judge.'.[64] I would delete 'almost' and go even further and say: the English barrister *is* a judge, functionally. Atiyah and Summers get closest to my point when they call the barrister 'a kind of embryonic judge'.[65]

---

[61] See, for example, Lord Chancellor's Department, *Judicial Statistics, England and Wales, for the Year 1994* 20 (Her Majesty's Stationery Office, Cm 2891, July 1995).

[62] Judicial Appointments Group, Lord Chancellor's Department, 'Judicial Appointments: The Lord Chancellor's Policies and Procedures' 5 (Lord Chancellor's Department, n.d.). See also Robert J. Martineau, *Appellate Justice in England and the United States: A Comparative Analysis* 65 (1990).

[63] *Judicial Statistics, England and Wales, for the Year 1994*, note 61 above, at 91.

[64] Atiyah and Summers, note 54 above, at 365.   [65] Id. at 367.

Above all, the barristers marshal the facts and the legal authorities for decision, which is half the work of a judge. Judges can trust the barristers to play straight with them concerning the facts and the cases and the other materials for judgment. This is the general belief of students of the English legal system,[66] and it is also what the judges I spoke to in England told me and what my own observations of appellate argument in the Court of Appeal confirmed.[67] Being drawn from the identical pool, moreover, judges and barristers can readily understand each other. They are on the same wavelength. As a result of these things, English judges are able to function without law clerks, who play an essential role in the American system with its effectively open bar dominated by lawyers whom the judges do not trust. American lawyers are called 'officers of the court', but this is said with a smile (or a sneer). Barristers really *are* officers of the court.[68] They are part-time judges and case filterers, as I have said, but most important they are the law clerks. That is not all they are, and it is not their own image of what they are, but it is a great deal of what they are, in part because the bulk of what American 'litigators' do—the preparation for trials that rarely occur, because the case is settled—is in England handled partly by solicitors rather than wholly by barristers.[69] On a recent visit to the United States, Lord Woolf of the Appellate Committee of the House of Lords is reported to have said (and he has confirmed

[66] See, for example, Maimon Schwarzschild, 'Class, National Character, and the Bar Reforms in Britain: Will There Always Be an England?' 9 *Connecticut Journal of International Law* 185, 196–197, 201 (1994).

[67] See Appendix B ('The Udu Case') at the end of this book.

[68] Though not called that. In England it is the *solicitors* who are the officers of the court. John O'Hare and Robert N. Hill, *Civil Litigation* 14, 16 (5th ed. 1990)

[69] See id. at 14–17; John Morison and Philip Leith, *The Barrister's World and the Nature of Law*, chs. 3–4 (1992); Quintin Johnstone and John A. Flood, 'Paralegals in English and American Law Offices' 2 *Windsor Yearbook of Access to Justice* 152 (1982); Schwarzschild, note 66 above, at 186, 230; and discussion and references in John F. Vargo, 'The American Rule on Attorney Fee Allocation: The Injured Person's Access to Justice' 42 *American University Law Review* 1567, 1603 (1993). Solicitors who work in the litigation department of their firms are often referred to as 'litigators' even if they do not appear in court. Americans also call lawyers who work on litigation yet may never (or very rarely) examine a witness or address a judge or jury 'litigators'. I am told that, until recently at least, solicitors did most of the work in preparing a case for trial even when the trial was handled by a barrister, and that they still do a great deal of that work.

to me the accuracy of the report) that he wanted the law lords to have law clerks *so that the judges could curtail the amount of time that they give barristers for oral argument*—which makes my point that barristers and law clerks are substitutes.

The United States has one staff of lawyers that corresponds to the English bar, and that is the staff of the Solicitor General of the United States. The Solicitor General handles all federal government litigation in the U.S. Supreme Court, and in addition must approve the taking of any appeal by the federal government from a lower to a higher court. Because the office is very small (about 20 lawyers), because its staff is salaried rather than paid on a contingent-fee or other incentive basis, and because it appears repeatedly before the same nine-person tribunal, it depends on the trust and good will of the judges to a far greater degree than is typical of American lawyers. The results show. The Solicitor General has been called 'The Tenth Justice'. His role in screening applications for Supreme Court review (and also appeals to the intermediate appellate courts) by the federal government[70] is quasi-judicial in character, and the briefs and arguments made by the members of the office are on average far more thoughtful, detached, and intellectually honest than those of private law firms.

Without a functional adjustment in the number of English and American judges and lawyers, the ratio of lawyers to judges in the two countries is virtually the same and is much higher than in the Continental legal systems, as we can see in Table 1.1.[71]

---

[70] The Court's jurisdiction is today almost entirely discretionary, and the Court accepts only about one percent of the total number of applications for review that it receives.

[71] The source for the first column in the table is an unpublished study by the Court Service, a unit of the Lord Chancellor's Department. The data for that study were obtained by the embassies of the United Kingdom in the countries studied, and are for 1994. The population statistics in the second column are from *World Factbook*, various years, except in the case of England, where the source is the *1995 Annual Abstract of Statistics* 4 (Central Statistical Office 1995) (tab. 2.1). The number of lawyers is from Marc Galanter, 'News from Nowhere: The Debased Debate on Civil Justice' 71 *Denver University Law Review* 77, 104-107 (1993). The population of Germany is the population of East Germany in 1990 plus the population of West Germany in 1985. The two populations were combined in order to enable the matching of Galanter's separate statistics for the two countries as they then were. The third column is simply the ratio of the first two columns.

Table 1.1 Judges, Lawyers, and Populations, in Different
Countries

Country	Ratio of Population to Full-time Judges	Ratio of Population to Lawyers	Ratio of Lawyers to Judges
Austria	4,700	3,154	1.49
Canada	17,000	600	28.31
Denmark	18,350	1,705	10.76
England	55,000	964	57.05
France	12,350	2,035	6.07
Germany	4,500	656	6.86
Italy	7,850	1,232	6.37
Japan	57,900	994	58.27
New Zealand	23,800	760	31.33
Spain	11,850	1,128	10.50
Switzerland	5,600	1,958	2.86
United States	19,900	365	54.59

Statistics such as these reinforce the prevalent impression of a distinctive Anglo-American legal system.

But if we add the number of barristers to the number of English judges, and the number of law clerks to the number of American judges, and then divide each sum by the number of lawyers in each country (solicitors in England, all practicing lawyers in the United States), the ratio of 'lawyers' to 'judges' is at least four times higher in the United States than in England. Computed in this manner, the English ratio—6.1 lawyers to 1 judge—is actually lower than the average (unweighted) of the Continental nations, which is 6.4 to 1, while the ratio of lawyers to judges in the United States remains much higher than the Continental ratios.[72] Even if each barrister were considered just

---

[72] Other sources, however, yield greater differences between the Continent and England (after adjusting the English figures) than the sources used to construct Table 1.1. For West Germany only, counting notaries as lawyers, a ratio of only 2 lawyers to 1 judge can be calculated for 1979-1981 from Alan N. Katz, 'Federal Republic of Germany' in *Legal Traditions and Systems: An International Handbook* 85, 91–93 (Alan N. Katz ed. 1986). The corresponding ratio for France

half a judge, the ratio of judges to lawyers would still be more than twice as high in England as in America, though it would be much lower than on the Continent. If we ask a slightly different question, the ratio of population to judges, it is (we see in Table 1.1) 19,900 to 1 in the United States and 4,500 to 1 in Germany; it would be 5,900 to 1 in England if barristers were counted as judges, a ratio much closer to the German than to the American.

A complicating factor is the system of magistrates. England has more than 30,000 magistrates (justices of the peace), all but a handful of whom are laymen and unpaid. A kind of cross between judges and jurors, they handle the vast majority of the lesser criminal cases as well as some family matters.[73] Were they counted as judges, the ratio of judges to lawyers in the English legal system would shoot up. But the number of magistrates would have to be drastically discounted, for they are part-timers; the average magistrate devotes only 10 per cent of his or her time to judicial duties. And if I counted magistrates in the total for English judges, I would have to count as judges American jurors, justices of the peace, and judges of traffic courts and domestic-relations courts. This would greatly increase the American ratio of judges to lawyers, even after the number of jurors was discounted to reflect their part-time status.

I keep harping on the ratio of judges to lawyers and the reader may wonder why that is such an important index to the character of a legal system. There are two reasons. The first is that a high ratio of judges to lawyers enables judges to do more in cases relative to what the lawyers do—to be more active and investigative, and less purely umpireal. It is thus a precondition to the 'inquisitorial' system that so distinguishes the Continental from the American judicial system, and that would I think be found characteristic of the English judicial system as well if barristers were considered a type of judge, for then trials and appeals would be dominated by judges rather than, as in America, by lawyers. Second, a high ratio of judges to lawyers

(excluding *juges d'instruction* but including *notaires*) is 18:1 (computed from Katz, 'France' in id. at 105, 112–115 [1982 figures]) and for Canada it is 23:1 (computed from statistics furnished me by the Canadian Centre for Justice Statistics).

[73] See *Judicial Statistics, England and Wales, for the Year 1994*, note 61 above, at 94.

encourages the emergence of a career judiciary, with its very different values, as we are about to see, from those of the non-career judiciary characteristic of the United States. The more judges there are relative to practicing lawyers, the more difficult it is to staff the judiciary by lateral entry. If, as a consequence, judges are hired when young, the higher positions are likely to be filled by promotion from within. And the larger a judiciary is (absolutely, not relative to the number of lawyers), the more formal and hierarchical its structure must be if the judges are to be effectively supervised and coordinated. The inquisitorial system and a career structure of the judiciary are related in another way. Because judges do more in an inquisitorial system than in an adversary system, they have to be technically more proficient.[74] They need to be better trained and more carefully selected and monitored, and these things are easier to achieve in a career service than in one based on lateral entry.

B. *A Career Judiciary*

Once we recognize that barristers are a form of judge, and then add to that the fact that almost all the higher-court judges in England are former barristers, and the further fact that almost all barristers have been barristers ever since they completed their education, we can see that in actuality England has a career judiciary. In this respect England is like the Continent and decidedly unlike the United States, where most entry into the judiciary still is lateral, though this is changing slowly. The careerist character of the English judiciary is confirmed by the promotion ladder (with its many rungs—assistant recorder, recorder, Queen's Counsel, deputy High Court judge, High Court judge, Court of Appeal judge, law lord) and reinforced by the virtual abolition of the civil jury, for the civil jury brings into the ranks of the American judiciary (jurors are lay judges) a host of complete amateurs. Moreover, most American judges— indeed, almost all except federal judges, and they are fewer than 10 per cent of the total even of judges who have a general jurisdiction—are elected rather than appointed. Elections are a

---

[74] John H. Langbein, 'The German Advantage in Civil Procedure' 52 *University of Chicago Law Review* 823 (1985).

method of selection inimical to the emergence of a competent career judiciary. Realistically, the English judiciary is far more bureaucratic—not in any invidious sense, but in a purely descriptive, Weberian sense[75]—than the American judiciary. In this respect it is again like the Continental judiciaries. And most barristers, like Continental judges, generally have no other university education except law. (This was not always true; barristers used to take their university degree in fields other than law.) Like military officers, they begin to separate themselves intellectually from the rest of the community at an earlier age than American judges.

If I am right that barristers are in a realistic though incomplete sense judges, this has damaging implications for proposals to 'deregulate' the English legal system. No one supposes that free entry into judging, like free entry into other professions and occupations, is unproblematic even as a matter of economic theory. I shall have more to say on this point in the third lecture.

A career judiciary is bound to be unlike the lateral-entry, rather political, rather amateurish, high-variance, non-hierarchical judiciary that one finds in the United States. Advancement in a career judiciary depends on merit evaluated in accordance with bureaucratic norms that emphasize obedience, integrity, diligence, discretion, and intelligence but not independence, flair, imagination, ideology (other than the ideology of conformity to bureaucratic norms), breadth of experience or knowledge, or diversity of social background or of racial or ethnic identity and other dimensions of representativeness.[76] A career judiciary tends to be homogeneous in values and preferences, narrowly professional, technically adept (as I have noted), and politically timid[77]—adding up to a mindset

---

[75] See John Bell, 'The Judge as Bureaucrat' in *Oxford Essays in Jurisprudence: Third Series* 33 (John Eekelaar and John Bell eds. 1987).

[76] How *anomalous* Lord Denning seemed among modern English judges; how at home he would have been in an American court system.

[77] For empirical evidence that a career judiciary may penalize judges who take unpopular political stances, see J. Mark Ramseyer and Eric B. Rasmusen, 'Judicial Independence in Civil Law Regimes: Econometrics from Japan' (University of Chicago Law School and Indiana University School of Business, unpublished, Nov. 15, 1995). On career judiciaries generally, see John Bell, 'Principles and Methods of Judicial Selection in France' 61 *Southern California Law*

highly congenial to legal positivism. The more alike judges are, moreover, the less conscious they will be of the contestability of the premises of decision.[78] They will see their function—rightly so, in a sense—as one of logical deduction, hence rigorous and non-political. The English judiciary, like that of the Continental nations, is extremely homogeneous.[79]

The fact that law is an undergraduate subject in England and on the Continent, and not in the United States, plays a role in this homogeneity. The 18-year-old who decides to study law is likely to be drawn from a relatively narrow band of the political and cultural spectrum, and he will not be much exposed to the extremist elements in university faculties. Americans go to law school only after undergoing four years of potentially radicalizing, or, perhaps more accurately, potentially polarizing, university education.

I do not want to exaggerate the positivism of English (or Continental) judges. Hart and Raz acknowledge, as we have seen, the 'legislative' role of judges. Bell's study of policy arguments in English decisions shows that English judges draw freely on considerations of policy to decide novel cases, both common law and statutory, and, occasionally, to overrule decisions.[80] We shall consider examples of English judicial creativity in Lecture Two. The difference along the aggressiveness-timidity spectrum between American and English judges is one of degree. But there is a difference, and though the formalism of Continental judges must not be exaggerated either,[81] the difference moves the English judges closer to their Continental than to their American counterparts.

Another relevant consequence of a career judiciary is to limit the length of term of the highest judges. They are at the top of a

---

Review 1757 (1988); David S. Clark, 'The Selection and Accountability of Judges in West Germany: Implementation of a Rechtsstaat' 61 Southern California Law Review 1797 (1988); J. Mark Ramseyer, 'The Puzzling (In)Dependence of Courts: A Comparative Approach' 23 Journal of Legal Studies 721 (1994).

[78] Simpson, note 30 above, at 98.
[79] Atiyah and Summers, note 54 above, at 353–356; Abel, note 55 above, at 74–85.
[80] John Bell, Policy Arguments in Judicial Decisions (1983).
[81] As emphasized in Mitchel de S.-O.-l'E. Lasser, 'Judicial (Self-) Portraits: Judicial Discourse in the French Legal System' 104 Yale Law Journal 1325 (1995).

ladder. It takes many years to climb the rungs. And in any bureaucracy there is pressure to have a low retirement age in order to provide promotion opportunities for the people climbing the ladder. So the term of the highest judges tends to be compressed at both ends. The older the age of appointment to a senior judicial position and the shorter the term, the less likely the judge is to prove to be an 'activist', for he will not have enough time to learn, master, and exploit a new role, that of judicial lawmaker.

It is no accident that we find career judiciaries in modern parliamentary systems. These systems, at least in the wealthy countries, are more centralized than the American, or the eighteenth-century English, system of government. Centralization makes it feasible for the legislature, which in England is controlled by the executive, to take the laboring oar in making rules and to reduce the judges to being primarily rule appliers. Because the 'government' (that is, the non-judicial branches) is more powerful than in the United States, the government's staff, the civil service, is more powerful, is taken more seriously, attracts better people, performs better, and so leaves less room for the judges to patch up its work. Most important, with the judges stripped of political functions, they really are technicians and it does not matter that they are unrepresentative of the population any more than it matters that engineers are unrepresentative. Being technicians, hence unrepresentative and politically inexperienced, they shudder at the thought of going into competition with Parliament and 'legislating'. So if they believe with Hart and Raz that they are legislating every time they decide a case the result of which is not foreordained by one of Raz's sources of law, they will leave the task of legal innovation to Parliament.

Bicameralism, the executive veto, the separate election of the legislators and the executive, federalism, and perhaps the individualistic and antistatist attitudes of the American people make American government weak from the standpoint of crisp and timely resolution of policy conflicts. A significant responsibility for what in other legal systems would be thought of as governing rather than adjudicating has fallen as it were by default to the judiciary. This does not mean that American judges are lawless, or that what they do when they are managing class actions, administering prison systems, renovating the common law, interpreting opaque statutes, or creating new constitutional rights is not law. It means only that judge-made law, the sort of law that makes legal positivists uncomfortable because its sources are so indistinct (why, some judges even on occasion find legal inspiration in economics), is a larger part of law in the United States than in most other—perhaps all other—countries. 'Law' means something different in the United States from what it means in England, consistent with my insistence that the word denotes a local rather than a universal concept.

American judges are either elected or, in the case of federal judges, appointed by the President and confirmed by the Senate.[82] Either way the judge has some democratic legitimacy, though it is indirect in the case of the appointed judges. Appointments to English courts below the House of Lords are made by the Lord Chancellor, and there is no confirmation. Judges so lacking in democratic legitimacy are unlikely to throw their political weight around. Guenter Treitel has offered the interesting speculation, which is very much in the spirit of my analysis, that English judges became less assertive as the franchise expanded, since with every advance of the democratic principle the non-representative character of the judiciary became more conspicuous.

The doctrinal conservatism of English judges has been said to be due in part to the loser-pays rule, which discourages the bringing of novel suits, since they are quite likely to fail and failure is more costly for a plaintiff than under the American rule.[83] The causation could easily run the other way, or both ways. A court that does not think its role is to innovate will have no 'demand' for innovative suits and therefore no wish to encourage their being brought.

I have said that American judges are more political than English judges and therefore more powerful. But it would be more accurate to say that they are more powerful when it comes

---

[82] States such as Massachusetts that have an appointed judiciary follow a similar pattern to the federal.

[83] J. Robert S. Prichard, 'A Systemic Approach to Comparative Law: The Effect of Cost, Fee, and Financing Rules on the Development of the Substantive Law' 17 *Journal of Legal Studies* 451, 465–466 (1988).

to making the rules by which society lives but less powerful when it comes to applying those rules:

At all stages of the proceedings before or at the trial or on appeal, at the actual trial or hearing, the English court [judge] plays a dominating, positive and interventionist role. The conduct of the proceedings then comes under the direct, immediate and overall control of the court which thus plays a pointed and practical role by the dialectical process of asking searching questions calling for immediate answers about any matters arising in the proceedings. This open intervention for the search for the truth, within the parameters of the proceedings as they are constituted, helps greatly to clarify, amplify or correct any points or questions raised by the parties or the court.[84]

This is a description that few American judges would apply to themselves. Their role in court is generally a more passive one. Political judges are less trusted than technician judges—and rightly so, for they are, on average, less competent and less disinterested. It is no accident that America, but not England or the rest of Europe, has a vast number of elected judges; or that America, but not England or the rest of Europe, has civil juries; or that American judges exert less control over the jury in criminal cases than English judges, who comment freely to the jury about the weight of the evidence; or that American lawyers are more independent of judges, less docile, than their European (including English) counterparts. Just as the political character of the legislative and executive branches of government fuels a demand for a non-political judiciary, so the political character of the American judiciary fuels a demand for an offsetting power center, such as the electorate, or a truly independent jury, or both. Once again the English judiciary lines up with the Continental and against the American.

If we think that the essence of the rule of law is not any or all of the specific doctrines associated with it (such as no retroactive criminal punishments) but an institution, namely the independent judiciary, it becomes interesting to note that the English (and Continental) and American judiciaries have different forms of dependence and independence. English judges are not checked by juries in most civil cases, or by the electorate; but they have less independence from their own judicial superiors,

---

[84] Jack I. H. Jacob, *The Fabric of English Civil Justice* 12 (1987).

from the Lord Chancellor (a Cabinet official, not an independent official like the Chief Justice of the United States), and from Parliament. The situation is roughly the same on the Continent (setting to one side the special problems of some of the Central and Eastern European nations). In which nation or group of nations is the rule of law more secure today? That is difficult to say. The net difference may be slight.

I acknowledge that there are many differences between the English and the Continental legal system. But there are also many differences among the legal systems of the different Continental nations; there is not, really, a single Continental legal system. All I claim is that the English judiciary appears to be more like the Continental system(s) than it is like the American. If this is at least approximately right, then comparison between the English and American judiciaries may be more than just an intramural issue within the 'Anglo-American' legal system. There may be no such system. Atiyah and Summers's distinguished book may be misnamed.

C. *Ships Passing in the Night?*

Some observers of the Hart-Dworkin debate think it a case of ships passing in the night—think that Hart was trying to propound a theory of law, and Dworkin a theory of judging. Hart and Raz are emphatic that these are not the same thing, since judges often must go outside of law to decide cases. But there is real disagreement, because Dworkin does not concede that judges have to go outside of law to decide even the most difficult cases.[85] I have tried to persuade you that Hart's view is congenial to a timid judiciary, which is what a career judiciary, the kind of judiciary one finds in Europe—including, I have argued, England—is likely to be,[86] while Dworkin's view is congenial to a bold judiciary, which being bold must defend

---

[85] See, for example, Dworkin, note 4 above, at 37–43.

[86] The clearest counter-example is the constitutional courts of Europe, especially the German and Hungarian, which are even more free-wheeling political courts than the U.S. Supreme Court. See generally David P. Currie, *The Constitution of the Federal Republic of Germany* 337–338 (1994); András Sajó, 'Reading the Invisible Constitution: Judicial Review in Hungary' 15 *Oxford Journal of Legal Studies* 253 (1995).

itself against accusations that it is legislating, not judging. But the disagreement dissolves if the debaters are seen as each describing his own legal system—the Anglo-Continental, or European, versus the American—rather than propounding a universal concept of law. It is no accident that today's foremost legal positivist in succession to Hart, Joseph Raz, lives and teaches in England.[87] Or that Lord Devlin, in propounding a version of legal positivism similar to Hart's, was writing against Louis Jaffe, an American law professor who had urged, rather presumptuously as it seems to me, English judges to act more like the judges of the Warren Court.[88]

Now we know why the concept of law is so elusive. Writers on jurisprudence treat it as a universal topic; they decontextualize it; yet actually it is local. Within the context of a specific legal system, with its own settled expectations concerning the judicial function, it is possible to pronounce a judicial decision 'lawless' because it relies on considerations or materials that the local culture rules out of bounds for judges. An English judge would be lawless if he brought into the decisional process the full range of considerations that an American judge might bring to a similar case. Just conceivably, an American judge would be lawless if he conceived his role as narrowly as an English judge.

I have been comparing the English and American legal systems at a high level of generality. In the next lecture I look at the two systems more closely by examining some modern English common law opinions, with particular reference to the role of economics in them relative to the role that economics plays in modern American cases. In the last lecture I again step back and offer general comparisons and assessments.

---

[87] But of course so does Dworkin (Hart's successor as professor of jurisprudence at Oxford), though only part of each year.

[88] Louis L. Jaffe, *English and American Judges as Lawmakers* (1969), discussed in Devlin, note 11 above, ch. 1.

Lecture Two:
The Common Law

In this lecture I examine some modern English judicial opinions in the two major fields of law that appear to be most alike in England and America. These are torts and contracts, though I shall glance in passing at damages law in general and at the law of property. I shall be casting one eye back to the discussion of positivism in the first lecture and one eye forward to the discussion of the legal culture at large in the third. But my especial concern will be with the question (which is related however to both the issue of positivism and the bearing of culture) to what extent the features of the opinions that I shall be discussing can be referred to the greater penetration of law by economics, or by a social scientific outlook generally, in America than in England. Obviously I cannot cover anything like the full range of tort and contract doctrines in the two legal systems.

I. TORTS

There is a very fine opinion by Lord Justice Denning in *Latimer* v. *A.E.C. Ltd*[1] decided by the Court of Appeal in 1952. Denning states the test for negligence with great brevity and lucidity:

It seems to me that the learned [trial] judge has fallen into error by assuming that it was sufficient to constitute negligence that there was a foreseeable risk which the defendants could have avoided by some measure or other, however extreme. That is not the law. It is always necessary to consider what measures the defendants could have taken and to say whether they could reasonably be expected of them . . . Here the employers knew that the floor was slippery and that there was some risk in letting the men work on it, but, still, they could not reasonably be expected to shut down the whole works and send all the

---

[1] [1952] 1 All E.R. 1302 (A.C.).

men home. In every case of foreseeable risk it is a matter of balancing the risk against the measures necessary to eliminate it.[2]

The test was usefully refined in the second *Wagon Mound* case, dealing with the question of slight risks. Lord Reid explained that 'it does not follow that, no matter what the circumstances may be, it is justifiable to neglect a risk of such a small magnitude. A reasonable man would only neglect such a risk if he had some valid reason for doing so: e.g., that it would involve considerable expense to eliminate the risk. He would weigh the risk against the difficulty of eliminating it.'.[3]

These are formulations with which most American judges would be comfortable. But they are less precise than the formula that Judge Learned Hand of the U.S. Court of Appeals for the Second Circuit had invented some years before *Latimer* and that is now known as the Hand formula.[4] The formula, algebraic in form, is $B < PL$, where B is the burden of precautions necessary to avoid an accident, P the probability that the accident will occur unless the precautions are taken, and L the magnitude of the loss that will result if the accident occurs. If the inequality is satisfied—that is, if the cost of the precautions is less than the expected accident cost[5]—the defendant is negligent; if the inequality is not satisfied he is not negligent.[6] Although the Hand formula is in principle quantifiable, thus far its main value for American tort law has been to sharpen thinking about negligence and to bring to the surface the economic logic that is implicit in the common law of negligence and of torts more broadly.[7] The Hand formula adds structure to what would otherwise be rather loose speculation as to how a reasonable

---

[2] [1952] 1 All E.R. 1305 (A.C.).

[3] *Wagon Mound (No. 2), Overseas Tankship (U.K.) Ltd* v. *Miller Steamship* [1966] 2 All E.R. 709, 718 (Privy Council).

[4] The formula was announced in *United States* v. *Carroll Towing Co.*, 159 F.2d 169, 173 (2d Cir. 1947). For a discussion of the reception of the formula by American courts, see Stephen G. Gilles, 'The Invisible Hand Formula' 80 *Virginia Law Review* 1015 (1994).

[5] The 'expected accident cost' is the cost of the accident, if it occurs, discounted (i.e., multiplied) by the probability that it will occur if the precautions are not taken.

[6] The formula can of course be applied to the plaintiff, if the issue is contributory or comparative negligence.

[7] See my book with William M. Landes, *The Economic Structure of Tort Law* (1987); also Gilles, note 4 above.

person would or would not act in particular circumstances. And if judges ever develop a taste for deciding cases on the basis of exact measurement rather than intuition, the formula will point them to what they should measure, namely B, P, and L, which when put into the relation shown by the formula can be seen to be the elements of cost-benefit analysis, applied to law.

I do not know how many English judges have heard of the Hand formula. But I think that if it were explained to them they would accept it as a fair description of the modern English law of negligence.[8] It resolves automatically and succinctly the issues presented in the *Latimer* and *Wagon Mound (No. 2)* cases. The cost of precautions (B in the Hand formula) is, as Lord Denning realized, as important a consideration as the risk of an accident if the precautions are not taken, and may indeed, if great enough, offset a high risk; while the slightness of the risk, as Lord Reid realized, is significant only in relation to the cost of avoiding it. (If you divide B and P by the same factor—say 10— the inequality is unaffected.) But I find it difficult to imagine an English judge of Hand's era, or indeed of today, attempting to algebraicize a body of law, as Hand did with negligence.

Learned Hand was a lawyer rather than an economist or any other kind of social scientist. His undergraduate education had been humanistic rather than scientific, and he received his legal education in the nineteenth century. But something in the legal culture of the United States enabled or permitted him, in 1947, before there was a law and economics movement, to attempt a reformulation of the negligence standard in recognizably economic terms. I do not suggest that Hand would have described what he was doing in those words. And I do not wish to exaggerate the influence of the Hand formula, which has as yet been mainly academic rather than judicial, though its academic influence has been extraordinary and its judicial influence is growing.[9] I claim only that the effort to recast legal standards in social scientific terms can be fruitful and that the Hand formula illustrates this.

---

[8] See Gilles, note 4 above, at 1027 n. 28; also Cento Veljanovski, 'Legal Theory, Economic Analysis and the Law of Torts' in *Legal Theory and Common Law* 215, 232–233 (William Twining ed. 1986); and cf. Stephen G. Gilles, 'Negligence, Strict Liability, and the Cheapest Cost-Avoider' 78 *Virginia Law Review* 1291 (1992).   [9] Again see Gilles, note 4 above.

That 'something in the legal culture' to which I just referred carries me back for a moment to Lecture One. Even if Denning's and Hand's formulations of the negligence standard are analytically the same, their tone is different, and the difference corresponds to the difference between the English and American legal cultures discussed in the first lecture. Denning's formulation (and Reid's, and Atkin's in *Donoghue* v. *Stevenson*, below) ties the concept of negligence to what is reasonable to expect and thus to the norms of the community. Those norms tell us when the victim of an accident should feel indignant at the injurer, and traditionally conceived the tort remedy is a substitute for private vengeance (a point to which I return in Lecture Three). Another name for community norms is custom, for legal positivists a proper source of law. Hand's formula recasts the negligence standard as a policy instrument for promoting the efficient allocation of resources. This is a 'legislative' conception remote from the positivistic thinking of English judges, as of Continental judges. As I noted in Lecture One, American judges are uniquely hospitable to social science, and the basic reason, I believe, is simply that the legislative or policymaking approach, which social science aids and abets, is congenial to American judges and *only* to American judges.

In Lecture One I associated positivism with formalism: it is merely an association. I acknowledged positivist Joseph Raz's emphatic repudiation of formalism, and we shall see throughout the present lecture that English common law decisions are often not formalistic at all. But I do think that they are more formalistic on average than American decisions, although rather than try to prove this I shall merely give an example. It is the recent decision by the House of Lords in *Rhone* v. *Stephens*.[10] In 1960 the owner of a house and attached cottage sold the cottage, promising in the deed of sale that he and succeeding owners of the house would maintain the common roof for the benefit of the buyer of the cottage and their successors. In 1986 the then owners of the cottage sued the then owners of the house to compel the latter to repair a leak in the part of the roof over the cottage. They lost. The court's reasoning was wooden, even though the economics of positive covenants had been discussed

[10] [1994] 2 All E.R. 65 (H.L.).

in a recent article by a well-known English law professor.[11] The court said that if the promise (covenant) in the deed had been negative—for example, a promise not to alter the roof—a breach of the promise would have been an attempt to enlarge the rights retained by the seller and would be enjoined. But since the promise was positive—to maintain the roof in good repair—to enforce the promise would be to impose a contractual obligation on one who had not signed any contract, namely the present owner of the house. I do not understand this. That present owner bought with knowledge of the covenant, because it was in the original deed. Why he should not be bound just as if he had signed the deed escapes me. There are economic objections to enforcing restrictive covenants that do not 'touch and concern' the land,[12] but the repair covenant did.

Let me return to negligence. The courts in both countries have been greatly vexed by the question whether liability for negligence should be confined to parties standing in a particular relation to the accident victim. Negligence is a failure to take due care, whether 'due care' is defined by the Hand formula or by more conventional formulations of the negligence standard. So the law of negligence is said to impose a 'duty' of due care, and the question is then whether the duty runs to everyone who might be endangered or just to some subset of the endangered. The most notable American decision on the question is *MacPherson* v. *Buick Motor Co.*,[13] written by Cardozo. It held that if through negligence the manufacturer of an automobile introduces a defect that injures the person who bought the automobile from the dealer, the manufacturer is liable to that person even though he had not bought the automobile directly from the manufacturer and therefore there was no contractual relation between them. The counterpart decision in England is *Donoghue* v. *Stevenson*[14] where the defect was the presence of a

[11] Bernard Rudden, 'Economic Theory v. Property Law: The *Numerus Clausus* Problem' in *Oxford Essays in Jurisprudence: Third Series* 239 (John Eekelaar and John Bell eds. 1987).
[12] Richard A. Posner, *Economic Analysis of Law* 69–70 (4th ed. 1992). The examples I give there are a promise not to sell goods or services in competition with the buyer and a promise to sell the buyer firewood at a low fixed price for twenty years. [13] 111 N.E. 1050 (N.Y. 1916).
[14] [1932] A.C. 562 (H.L.).

snail in a bottle of ginger beer. The outcome was the same as in *MacPherson*. But where Cardozo had been content to assimilate the automobile to the class of dangerous articles, a recognized exception to the principle that manufacturers were not liable to persons with whom they had no contractual relation, Lord Atkin began by setting forth a general principle to determine the scope of the duty of care:

You must take reasonable care to avoid acts or omissions which you can reasonably foresee would be likely to injure your neighbour. Who, then, in law is my neighbour? The answer seems to be—persons who are so closely and directly affected by my act that I ought reasonably to have them in contemplation as being so affected when I am directing my mind to the acts or omissions which are called in question.[15]

This formulation unfortunately does not have a very precise content, and in applying it to the snail in the bottle of ginger beer Lord Atkin emphasized two points that do not bear a clear relation to the neighbor principle. The first is that the consumer cannot inspect the bottle before purchase and, realistically, cannot be expected to discover the snail until too late. The second point is that unless the bottle was sold with a warranty from either the retailer or the manufacturer, the consumer would be without a remedy if the duty concept were held to bar her suit. The points are linked, but nevertheless weak. The fact that the purchaser cannot inspect before use is a reason for believing that the product will be sold with a warranty, in which event the purchaser will not be without a remedy. The bottle of ginger beer had been bought 'for' the victim by a friend,[16] and there is no discussion of whether there was a warranty accompanying the sale and if so whether it extended to her. The rest of Lord Atkin's very long opinion is taken up with a discussion of the precedents. The weight of precedent was against liability, but he was able to show, though only with the help of some rather hair-splitting distinctions,[17] that no actual holding stood in the way of imposing liability on the manufacturer of the ginger beer.

---

[15] [1932] A.C. 580 (H.L.).   [16] Id. at 562.
[17] Notably of *Winterbottom* v. *Wright* 10 M. & W. 109, 152 Eng. Rep. 402 (Ex. 1842), which had been understood to establish a requirement of privity of contract for products liability. *Winterbottom* is discussed at [1932] A.C. 588–589.

Neither Cardozo nor Atkin offered a practical reason for liability, such as the burden on the courts if the consumer sues the retailer for breach of warranty and the retailer then brings in the manufacturer as a third-party defendant, seeking indemnification on the basis of the manufacturer's warranty to the retailer, or the possibility that the retailer is judgment-proof. Both *MacPherson* and *Donoghue* are dogmatic opinions and laid unstable foundations for further judicial explorations of the 'duty limitation' on liability.

The tendency in both our countries has been to relax the limitation and thus extend liability, notably to investors misled by company auditors' reports, though the investors are not in a contractual relation with the auditors.[18] I want to skip over those cases and come to *White* v. *Jones*.[19] A man of 78 who had cut his daughters out of his will decided to reinstate them and instructed his solicitors to draw up a new will. The solicitors dilly-dallied and when he died two months later the new will had not yet been prepared, so the daughters got nothing, and they sued the solicitors. The House of Lords held that the solicitors were liable in tort to the daughters for negligence, even though the solicitors' contract had been with the deceased alone. In justifying this result Lord Goff relied almost entirely on what he called 'the impulse to do practical justice . . . If such a duty is not recognized, the only persons who might have a valid claim (ie the testator and his estate) have suffered no loss, and the only person who has suffered loss (ie the disappointed beneficiary) has no claim.'.[20]

Lord Goff's emphasis on practical justice chimes in with an address that he had given some years earlier to the British Academy, in which in contrast to Lord Devlin he had said that

the most potent influence upon a court in formulating a statement of legal principle . . . is the desired result in the particular case before the court . . . When we talk about the desired result, or the merits, of any

---

[18] Recently, however, a mood of retrenchment has become perceptible in the English case law concerning auditors' liabilities. See, for example, *Caparo Industries PLC* v. *Dickman* [1990] 2 A.C. 605 (H.L.). A parallel mood has resulted very recently in legislation in the United States curtailing auditors' liability in suits under the federal securities laws. See Private Securities Litigation Reform Act of 1995, 109 Stat. 737.   [19] [1995] 1 All E.R. 691 (H.L.).

[20] Id. at 702.

particular case, we can do so at more than one level. There is the crude, purely factual level—the plaintiff is a poor widow, who has lost her money, and such like. At another level there is the gut reaction, often most influential. But there is a more sophisticated, lawyerly level, which consists of the perception of the just solution in legal terms, satisfying both the gut and the intellect.[21]

The poor widow enters rather unmistakably into Lord Goff's speech in *White* v. *Jones*, for he notes evidence that (and this of course is entirely plausible) solicitors' mistakes are most likely in the handling of modest estates, 'with the result that it tends to be people of modest means, who need the money so badly, who suffer.'.[22] But this and the other points that Lord Goff makes in support of imposing liability on the solicitors to the intended legatees are the buttresses rather than the vault. The animating principle is that someone injured through the negligence of another should be able to obtain damages.

But there is a competing principle, perhaps one more obvious to an economist than to a lawyer, though it is mentioned in Lord Mustill's dissent and also in Lord Nolan's speech concurring with Lord Goff, that *White* v. *Jones* violates. This is that, in assessing the appropriateness of a remedy, its *total* consequences must be considered. The argument against awarding damages in 'economic loss' cases, such as a case in which the defendant's negligence obstructs access to the plaintiff's retail store, is that the plaintiff's loss may very well be a gain to a competitor, to whom the plaintiff's customers are diverted by the obstruction. In that event the net social loss imposed by the obstruction may be much less than the loss to the plaintiff, and may even be zero.[23] *White* v. *Jones* is similar. The effect of

---

[21] Robert Goff, 'Maccabean Lecture in Jurisprudence: The Search for Principle' 69 *Proceedings of the British Academy* 169, 183 (1983).

[22] [1995] 1 All E.R. at 702.

[23] See Landes and Posner, note 7 above, at 251–255. It is unlikely to be zero, as David Friedman has pointed out to Landes and me. The other store is likely to be less efficient than the plaintiff, or operating at full capacity, or less convenient for some customers; otherwise it might have had the business of the plaintiff's customers already. So the diversion will probably increase the total costs of serving those customers (including travel and other costs borne directly by the customers). It should be noted that *White* v. *Jones* is an exception to the general position of the English courts, which is to deny recovery in economic loss cases. See John Bell, *Policy Arguments in Judicial Decisions* 57–60 (1983); B. S. Markesinis and S. F. Deakin, *Tort Law* 83–118 (3d ed. 1994).

imposing full liability on the solicitors for the loss to the intended legatees was to augment the estate and thus confer a windfall on the deceased's survivors. For if the will had been changed, the legatees in the previous will would have taken less, or nothing. As a result of the imposition of liability on the solicitors, those legatees get to keep what they got, even though by hypothesis the deceased did not want them to get that much, or perhaps anything.

The ideal solution[24] in my hypothetical case of the obstructed store would be to make the store that had gained from the obstruction disgorge its gain to the plaintiff. But that is not a very feasible remedy, and it would be wholly impracticable if the lost business of the plaintiff had gone to several stores rather than one. So it is best for the judges to let the loss lie where it has fallen, comforted by the knowledge that the plaintiff could have insured himself against such a loss, and perhaps did. It is easier to devise a workable solution in the solicitors' case: reform the will, so that the original legatees are made to transfer their legacies (or so much of those legacies as necessary to carry out the deceased's intentions) to the intended legatees; and if this causes any inconvenience to the original legatees—they may have altered their position in reliance on having received the legacies—give them a claim against the solicitors. That claim would be the measure of the net social loss from the solicitors' negligence, and awarding that much and no more would thus avoid both under- and over-compensation. This possibility is not discussed in *White* v. *Jones*. Would it be too radical for an English court? Not necessarily. The familiar concept of fraudulent conveyance would provide a handhold by way of analogy. My court recently had a case in which charities received, all unknowingly, donations from a man who had obtained the money for the donations through securities fraud; and we held that, since the charities had not given consideration for the donations (any more than the original beneficiaries in *White* v. *Jones*), they must give it back.[25] Even more to the point, the Court of Appeal had held many years earlier that a testator's

---

[24] Well, almost ideal. See previous footnote.
[25] *Scholes* v. *Lehmann*, 56 F.3d 750 (7th Cir. 1995).

next of kin could recover the money paid by his executors by mistake to charities.[26]

Lord Goff did not respond directly to Lord Mustill's alarming suggestion that the logic of the majority's position was that if the new will had been drawn up in timely fashion and a careless driver had killed the deceased en route to the execution of the will, the driver would be liable to the intended legatees. There is a difference, though. When asked to redraw the will with specified legacies for the daughters, the solicitors were of course placed on notice of the exact amount of their potential liability; the driver would not be on notice. There is, however, an argument not alluded to in any of the opinions in *White* v. *Jones* that this should not matter. The argument is that since, by definition, a careless driver should take more care, his liability should not be affected by how much harm his carelessness did. The solicitors should not have needed the threat of being held liable to intended beneficiaries of a client's will to avoid negligently harming the client, and had they done their duty to their client they would not have been in danger of being subjected to 'crushing' or 'unforeseeable' liability. If this is right, there is very little to the duty limitation; but there are some not entirely satisfactory reasons for believing that it is wrong.[27] I do not want to get into that question here, though I shall be glancing at it later, when I discuss punitive damages. I merely want to flag it as the kind of question that, along with insistence on taking account of *all* the effects of a remedy, is given salience by the economic approach to tort law. Although there is much to criticize in American law, it is a strength of that law that it is open to the approaches of other disciplines and in particular to that of economics.

It is true that by making the solicitors in *White* v. *Jones* liable for the full extent of the daughters' loss rather than for just the social cost of the solicitors' negligence, the court created a

---

[26] In *re Diplock's Estate*, [1948] 2 All E.R. 318 (A.C.), aff'd sub nom. *Ministry of Health* v. *Simpson* [1951] A.C. 251 (H.L.). The mistake arose from the fact that the direction in the will, giving the executors absolute discretion to designate the charitable recipients of the bequest, was void for vagueness and should therefore have been ignored.

[27] I explore these reasons in my opinion in *Edwards* v. *Honeywell, Inc.*, 50 F.3d 484 (7th Cir. 1995).

greater incentive for solicitors to be careful. But the question whether to make a tortfeasor liable for more than the harm he causes is similar to—from a functional or economic standpoint identical to—the question whether to impose punitive on top of compensatory damages, to which the usual English answer is 'no', as we shall see shortly.

I want to illustrate my point about the greater receptivity of American law to economic arguments further with reference to two issues in the law of tort damages. The first concerns what is called the 'loss of a chance'. The plaintiff in *Hotson* v. *East Berkshire Area Health Authority*[28] injured his hip in a fall and received incompetent treatment in the defendant's hospital. The hip became severely deformed. The judge determined that the fall itself had created a 75 per cent probability that the plaintiff would develop the deformity and that the hospital's negligence had made that a certainty. So he computed the plaintiff's loss from the deformity and awarded him 25 per cent of that loss as his damages. The House of Lords reversed. Their lordships opined that the issue of the proper amount of damages could not be reached unless there was a finding that the defendant's negligence had caused the injury for which damages were sought, that is, the deformity of the hip. The issue of causation was to be resolved by balancing the probabilities. The trial judge had done this and found that the balance inclined against a finding that the negligence of the hospital had been the cause of the injury. Therefore the hospital was not liable. This reasoning is wooden. We can see this by glancing back at *White* v. *Jones*. It was only probable, not certain, that the plaintiffs would have been better off had the solicitors acted. For the deceased might have changed his mind again and decided not to execute the new will. A loss is still a loss even if it is only probable, as are most things in life. This is clearly recognized in figuring damages for loss of future earnings in cases of death or disability: the damages are calculated with reference to life expectancy, and thus are probablistic. Hotson would have paid a lot (if he had had a lot to pay) for a 25 per cent chance of avoiding a crippling deformity. This shows, at least to an economist, who frequently measures 'value' by willingness to pay (or by reservation price—

[28] [1987] 2 All E.R. 909 (H.L.).

the lowest price at which the owner of a good would part with it), that Hotson lost something by being deprived of that chance.

Even though it is more likely than not that the hospital's negligence was *not* responsible for the deformity, that negligence deprived the plaintiff—with a 100 per cent probability—of a valuable though intangible asset, namely a 25 per cent chance of avoiding a serious loss. I do not understand why that loss should not be compensable. If it is not, there will be a tendency to undercompensate systematically the victims of medical and other accidents (accidental emission of radiation is another good example) that create significant probabilities of serious injury but well short of 50 per cent. Not all American courts understand this, but many do[29] and the rest could, I think, be brought round if the economics of the situation were made clear to them.

But a qualification is necessary. If damages for loss of a chance are awarded, it is essential that the courts do so consistently and thus *not* award a plaintiff 100 per cent of his damages when all that he has proved is a 51 per cent probability that he was injured. Otherwise there will be overcompensation. Many American courts do not understand this; and if it were thought too complicated to make the lost chance the standard of recovery in all cases, or at least all cases in which there was a substantial doubt about the causal relation between the plaintiff's injury and the tort, this would be an argument against the lost-chance award. Maybe this is what the House of Lords had in mind, but it did not say so.

My second example from the law of tort damages is *Rookes* v. *Barnard*,[30] a House of Lords decision that sharply limited the situations in which punitive damages can be awarded and that has been followed in later cases.[31] The plaintiff lost his job

[29] See, for example, *Brown* v. *Doll*, 75 F.3d 1200, 1205–1207 (7th Cir. 1996); *Delaney* v. *Cade*, 873 P.2d 175, 186–187 (Kan, 1994); *McKellips* v. *Saint Francis Hospital, Inc.*, 741 P.2d 467, 475–477 (Okla. 1987); *Herskovits* v. *Group Health Cooperative*, 664 P.2d 474 (Wash. 1983); Joseph H. King, Jr., 'Causation, Valuation, and Chance in Personal Injury Torts Involving Preexisting Conditions and Future Consequences' 90 *Yale Law Journal* 1353 (1981).

[30] [1964] 1 All E.R. 367 (H.L.).

[31] See, for example, *AB* v. *South West Water Services Ltd* [1993] 1 All E.R. 609 (A.C.).

because the union from which he had resigned threatened a strike (in violation of the members' contracts of employment) against his employer unless the employer fired him. This was held to be a tort, and obviously a deliberate one, but their lordships held that the plaintiff could not be awarded punitive ('exemplary') damages. Lord Devlin, who gave the leading speech on the question, explained that the trier of fact could, in determining the *compensatory* damages to which the plaintiff was entitled, 'take into account the motives and conduct of the defendant where they aggravate the injury done to the plaintiff.'.[32] In saying this he was echoing Holmes's dictum that even a dog distinguishes between being kicked and being stumbled over.[33] After reviewing the cases, however, Lord Devlin concluded that the common law of England allowed the award of *punitive* damages in only two classes of case: 'oppressive, arbitrary or unconstitutional action by the servants of the government' and cases 'in which the defendant's conduct has been calculated by him to make a profit for himself which may well exceed the compensation payable to the plaintiff.'.[34] The plaintiff's case fell within neither class, so he could not receive an award of punitive damages.

Lord Devlin's second class is easy to understand: unless the defendant is forced to disgorge his profit, he will not be deterred by the threat of a tort action. The first class, based as it is on an absolute distinction between public and private action, seems arbitrary. The only justification offered is that 'the servants of the government are also the servants of the people and the use of their power must always be subordinate to their duty of service.'.[35] I get nothing from such a 'reason'.

Lord Devlin did not suggest that precedent foreclosed the award of punitive damages in cases falling outside his two classes, so we must consider why he wanted to confine awards so. The reason he offered was that it is the business of tort law to compensate, and of criminal law to deter. Why this should be so is not explained. Lord Devlin treats it as a self-evident proposition, which it is not. In particular it is hard to see how as

---

[32] [1964] 1 All E.R. at 407.
[33] Oliver Wendell Holmes, Jr., *The Common Law* 3 (1881).
[34] [1964] 1 All E.R. at 410.   [35] Id.

a practical matter the criminal law can be relied upon to deter most negligence—and negligence is the cause of most avoidable accidents—or even the type of intentional injury illustrated by *Rookes* v. *Barnard* itself. There is an internal inconsistency as well. Lord Devlin's insistence that it is not the job of tort law to deter is inconsistent with his recognition of the propriety of awarding punitive damages in his second class of case. To award a plaintiff more than he has lost, namely the defendant's profit, which by hypothesis exceeds the harm that the defendant has done to the plaintiff, is to give the plaintiff a windfall and thus violate the compensation principle. Granted there are alternative rationales to deterrence for awarding punitive damages. Indignation at the wrongdoer's being allowed to profit from his wrong is one. But the only one that Lord Devlin so much as hints at is deterrence: 'exemplary damages can properly be awarded whenever it is necessary to teach a wrongdoer that tort does not pay.'.[36]

If deterrence were brought to the forefront of analysis, as an economist would be inclined to do because of his interest in the creation of incentives to avoid inefficient behavior, an argument could be made for confining the award of punitive damages to cases in which the defendant's 'profit', broadly understood (as did Lord Devlin) to include non-pecuniary as well as pecuniary gains, exceeded the defendant's loss—which is to say to cases in Lord Devlin's second class. For in the generality of other cases the award of compensatory damages should be sufficient to deter. By hypothesis these are cases in which the defendant gains less from his tortious act than the plaintiff loses, so that if forced to compensate the plaintiff for the latter's loss the defendant will have incurred a net cost by his act.

A qualification is necessary. If the act is the sort that is difficult to detect or prove, as when a driver leaves the scene of an accident and is not identified, the defendant may have a net *expected* gain, after discounting the plaintiff's loss by the probability that he can establish the defendant's liability, from the tortious act. On this basis an economist would be inclined to recommend that in calculating the optimal damages for a tort, the harm done by the defendant should be divided by the

---

[36] [1964] 1 All E.R. at 411.

probability that the defendant will in fact be compelled to compensate the plaintiff. D should be set equal to L/P, where P is the probability just discussed, D the damages awarded, and L the plaintiff's loss. If P is smaller than one, D will exceed L. The difference will be a punitive component of the award. For example, if the harm caused by the accident is $100 but the probability of the injurer's being made to pay for the harm is only .5, the damages award should be $200. This award will create an expected cost equal to the harm ($200 × .5 = $100). Of the $200 award, half is the punitive component, since the victim's actual damages are only $100.[37]

In later cases Lord Devlin's second class—a class that if qualified as I have just suggested would cover most cases in which a strong economic argument for awarding punitive damages could be made—has been defined exceedingly narrowly.[38] The reason seems to be the felt 'anomaly' of imposing punishment in a civil case. But the reason it is anomalous is never very fully explained and the proposition, I have emphasized, is not self-evident.

An argument can be made that the lack of any ceiling on the amount of punitive damages that can be awarded (unlike the usual criminal fine) injects an undesirable uncertainty into the decision-making of potential defendants. This argument, it turns out, raises the same issue as the 'duty limitation' that I discussed earlier.[39] By definition, the defendant could have avoided liability by doing what the law required him to do, namely avoid deliberate wrongdoing; so what is the harm in throwing the book at him? There are several answers, including the risk of a mistaken determination of wrongdoing (an answer also available to the question, why limit the duty of care to some circumscribed set of potential plaintiffs?). But these are not serious problems if punitive damages are confined, as I think they probably should be, to Lord Devlin's second class of cases. For that class has a built-in ceiling on the amount of punitive damages—namely the profit to the defendant from his tortious

[37] On the economics of punitive damages, see Landes and Posner, note 7 above, at 160–163.
[38] See Alan Reed, 'The End of the Line for Exemplary Damages?' 143 *New Law Journal* 929 (1993).
[39] This is an illustration of how economic analysis can uncover the analytical connections between seemingly unrelated legal doctrines.

act—that is not likely to be greatly increased by adopting the formula $D = L/P$. Most tortious acts are not concealable or at any rate not concealed, and therefore D will rarely exceed L by much.

If I correctly follow the drift of the case law since *Rookes* v. *Barnard*, Lord Devlin's second class has been allowed to shrivel up because of an inarticulate sense of the anomalousness of punitive damages. So once again I make bold to suggest, no doubt with the same presumptuousness with which I taxed Professor Jaffe in my first lecture, that the English common law of torts could be improved by bringing economics to bear on it.

Rookes v. *Barnard* illustrates the tendency of conventional legal thinking to be excessively dichotomous. The conventional legal thinker draws an extremely sharp line between civil law and criminal law and between torts and contract. This tendency is due in part to failing to take a functional approach. Functionally, civil and criminal law alike, and tort and contract law alike, 'price' conduct that the law wishes to discourage or at least regulate. The optimal price will sometimes exceed the harm to the victim. If in a case where it does the more efficient method of fixing such a price is by awarding punitive damages on top of compensatory damages, rather than by locking the defendant up, the economist has great difficulty seeing why the award of punitive damages should be thought anomalous.

Another way to understand the difference between legal and economic thinking harks back to the discussion of the question 'What is law?' in Lecture One. The idea that criminal law is about deterrence and civil law about compensation is a product of the same kind of conceptual or essentialist thinking that underlies efforts to define the word 'law'. The alternative to thinking of civil law and criminal law, or tort and contract, as concepts is to think of them as tools. Economics encourages such a shift of focus, and by doing so can help to remove the blinders that judges sometimes wear.

II. CONTRACTS

I move now from a spotty examination of recent tort law to an even spottier one of recent contract law. I begin with another issue in which the American law was set on its modern course by Cardozo. The issue is substantial performance, and the American case, which held that defective performance of a building contract does not entitle the purchaser to insist that the defect be rectified if the cost would be disproportionate to the reduction in value caused by the defect, is *Jacob & Youngs, Inc.* v. *Kent*.[40] A recent English case dealing with the issue is *Ruxley Electronics & Construction Ltd.* v. *Forsyth*.[41] The defendant in *Ruxley* contracted to build a swimming pool for the plaintiffs that was to be 7 feet 6 inches deep at its deepest point. After the pool had been built the plaintiffs discovered that it was only 6 feet 9 inches deep at its deepest point and only 6 feet deep at the point where people would dive into the pool. The plaintiffs were awarded some damages, but less than the cost of rebuilding the pool to the contractually specified depth, which was what they had sought. The House of Lords held that they were not entitled to the cost of rebuilding because it would be disproportionate to the diminution in the market value of their property as a result of the breach. In fact that diminution was found to be zero—a bit implausibly, but maybe the fact that the shallower pool would be cheaper to operate and maintain would for most buyers have offset the loss of pleasure in its use. The damages that were awarded were intended merely to compensate the plaintiffs for the loss of personal pleasure that the plaintiffs suffered by not getting the depth of pool that they had wanted; it was now too shallow to dive into. Loss of pleasure had not been an issue in *Jacob & Youngs*. The breach of contract had involved the installation of the wrong brand of water pipe. The pipe was concealed in the walls and the wrong brand was just as good as the one that had been specified in the contract; so the damages really were zero.

The plaintiffs in *Ruxley* argued that the common law did not allow for such an award, and therefore they should get either nothing or the cost of rebuilding. The boldness of the argument is appealing.

Lord Bridge's brief speech is notable for his remark that 'since the populist image of the geriatric judge, out of touch with the real world, is now reflected in the statutory presumption of

---

[40] 129 N.E. 889 (N.Y. 1921).   [41] [1995] 3 All E.R. 268 (H.L.).

judicial incompetence at the age of 75, this is the last time I shall speak judicially in your Lordships' House. I am happy that the occasion is one when I can agree with your Lordships still in the prime of judicial life who demonstrate so convincingly that common sense and the common law here go hand in hand.'.[42] The other speeches wrestle with the thorny issues presented by the case. Although the award of damages for the loss of amenity seems the happy medium between zero and the cost of rebuilding, the assessment of such 'subjective' damages is obviously fraught with uncertainty. If the taste reflected in the contractual specification is idiosyncratic, any award of damages for 'the loss truly suffered by the promisee',[43] as Lord Mustill put it in his speech, is likely to be arbitrary.

His lordship used the economist's concept of 'consumer surplus' to sharpen the issue. The consumer surplus generated by the sale of a product is the area under a demand curve between that curve and the product's price. Demand curves, which express the relation between the price and the quantity of a product, are downward-sloping, reflecting the fact that buyers will pay more when a product is scarce than when it is abundant.[44] If the product is sold under competitive conditions, the area between the demand curve and the price, which is to say the amount of consumer surplus, is likely to be very large, as shown in Figure 1 (where the area labeled 'CS' is the consumer surplus); and it is a measure of the benefit that the consumers of the product, as a group, obtain from being able to buy the product at the competitive price. If swimming pools are sold in a competitive market, consumers will value the pools more than the price. That is, *most* consumers will. At the intersection of demand and price will be found the marginal consumer, who values the pool at just what it cost him; he obtains no consumer surplus.

So the swimming pool that the plaintiffs in *Ruxley* wanted would probably, though for the reason just given not certainly,

---

[42] [1995] 3 All E.R. at 271.   [43] Id. at 277.

[44] The assumption is that the product is sold at the same price to all customers—that is, that the seller or sellers do not discriminate in price. With perfect price discrimination, the demand curve would be the schedule of prices, so there would be no consumer surplus.

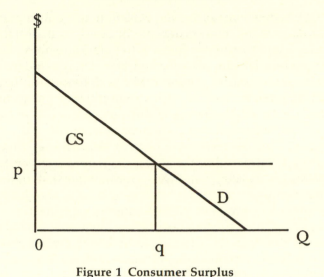

Figure 1 Consumer Surplus

have conferred on them a non-pecuniary benefit—remember that the market price of their property was unaffected by the substitution of the shallower pool for the one they had ordered—in excess of its price. They did get *a* pool, so the real loss was the difference between the consumer surplus that the desired pool would have conferred and the consumer surplus that the substituted pool conferred.

The difficulty, as Lord Mustill pointed out, is that consumer surplus is very difficult to measure. One of its essential parameters, the demand curve, is a schedule of hypothetical rather than real prices. And consumer surplus is an aggregation of the subjective values (net of price) that *all* consumers derive from the product and the aggregate may be easier to estimate than the surplus obtained by one of the consumers, the plaintiff in a suit. The downward slope of the demand curve suggests that the amount of surplus may vary greatly among consumers and approach or even reach zero for some of them.

I do not suggest that the concept of consumer surplus is essential either to Lord Mustill's speech or to the doctrine that it and the other speeches in the case adopt. Its use is merely another illustration of how economic thinking can sharpen legal concepts. It does not solve the problem that the case presents. The problem is less the uncertainty of damages than the likely consequence of that uncertainty. When damages are uncertain, courts (especially when no jury is in the picture) tend to err on the downside, because the plaintiff has the burden of proof. I would expect this tendency to operate strongly in a juryless English court when damages are sought for the loss of subjective value in building contractor cases in which the breach of contract does not reduce the market value of the property.[45] The damages awarded in the *Ruxley* case were a rather modest £2,500 (about $4,000), although I cannot call that figure un- reasonably low.

There is an argument for offering the plaintiff a choice between the court's estimation of his subjective loss and the saving to the contractor from the breach. Imagine a case in which the 'real', unknowable subjective loss is $500, the saving to the contractor $400 from having broken the contract, and the damages that the court would award for the plaintiff's subjective loss (the £2,500 in *Ruxley*) only $300. A contractor who correctly foresees the outcome of a suit will know that he can 'earn' $100 by the breach. This contractor's temptation to break his promise will be discouraged if the court offers the plaintiff the alternative that I have suggested. That seems a better solution than the draconian remedy proposed by the plaintiff in the *Ruxley* case,[46] a remedy that fails to consider the inevitability of minor breaches of building contracts.[47] Mine is a distinctly second-best remedy, however, because it assumes that there is no loss of

[45] If there were such a reduction, the court might be more generous in adding on damages for loss of subjective values, feeling that there was a solid basis for the suit. There is an analogy to the old rule that courts would not award damages for emotional distress unless the plaintiff had suffered a physical harm as well.

[46] In my hypothetical case, this might be $1,000 to rebuild the pool, an amount greatly in excess of the plaintiff's real loss of $500.

[47] As explained in Todd D. Rakoff, 'The Implied Terms of Contracts: Of "Default Rules" and "Situation-Sense" ' in *Good Faith and Fault in Contract Law* 191, 209 (Jack Beatson and Daniel Friedmann eds. 1995), the function of much of the detail in a building contract is 'not to express a purpose, or even "whim", of the owner but, rather, to serve as communication from the architect to the builder; details are commonly changed on the authority of the architect throughout the construction process'.

consumer surplus. It is a restitutionary remedy designed to deter fraud rather than to compensate a buyer for a loss.

Although *Ruxley* leaves some loose ends dangling, I cannot say that English contract law is behind American law in conforming to the principles of economics. It may be ahead of it. (I stress 'may'; it would be irresponsible of me to affirm the economic superiority of English to American contract law without a much fuller canvass and comparison than I have attempted, or could attempt within the compass of these lectures.) Consider the English courts' rejection of a general concept of 'unconscionability' or 'inequality in bargaining power' as grounds for refusing to enforce contracts, and, the same point differently expressed, their refusal to extend the defense of duress to cases in which a 'stronger' party refuses to deal with a 'weaker', to the latter's harm.[48] Inequality of bargaining power has no standing in economics as a basis for refusing to enforce a contract.[49] I also instance what appears to be the English courts' increasingly relaxed attitude toward penal and forfeiture provisions in contracts.[50] There are good economic reasons for such provisions, as well as a general economic presumption in favor of freedom of contract, and the economic reasons that have been offered against these provisions are not impressive.[51]

In acknowledging that England may have a more efficient body of contract law than America, do I refute my general thesis, that economics has penetrated law more deeply in America than in England and that American law is the better for this penetration? No; the English judges may have rejected economically unsound doctrines such as unconscionability not because they were economically unsound but because they were new. This would be consistent with my analysis in Lecture One of the different taste for innovation of English and American

[48] See, for example, *Hart* v. *O'Connor* [1985] 2 All E.R. 880 (Privy Council); *CTN Cash & Carry Ltd* v. *Gallaher Ltd* [1994] 4 All E.R. 714 (A.C.); A. H. Angelo and E. P. Ellinger, 'Unconscionable Contracts: A Comparative Study of the Approaches in England, France, Germany, and the United States' 14 *Loyola of Los Angeles International and Comparative Law Journal* 455, 460–472 (1992).

[49] See Posner, note 12 above, at 113–117.

[50] See P. S. Atiyah, *An Introduction to the Law of Contract* 452–457 (4th ed. 1989).   [51] See Posner, note 12 above, at 128–130.

judges. But more may be involved. In the most recent edition of Professor Atiyah's textbook on contract law—but it is already seven years old—we read that:

the pendulum has been swinging vigorously back to the ideology of freedom of contract, and it has become essential for teachers and students of contract law to assess the effects and implications of all this political and economic activity . . . Some introduction to economic arguments has become imperative for a book on the law of contract, even an introductory book like this. So this edition gives much greater prominence to the function of contract law as an instrument of economic exchange, and economic arguments are canvassed over a wide range of issues.[52]

Atiyah carries through on this promise by discussing a number of issues in contract law in explicitly economic terms. His approach forms a sharp contrast to the brief, impacted discussions of the economic approach that one finds in the English tort texts.[53] Notice that Atiyah attributes the trend toward economic liberalism that he finds in recent English cases to the reviving belief in free markets, a revival that has both influenced and been influenced by the rise of economic analysis of contract law.

But we should not be surprised, quite apart from academic fashions, to find common law judges reaching results that make good economic sense. It has been argued for many years, often with reference to classic English cases in torts and contracts, that the common law can best be understood by assuming counterfactually that the judges were *trying* to maximize economic efficiency.[54] There is even a theoretical reason, unrelated to the law and economics movement, to expect England to have a more efficient common law of contracts than the United States. Remember that *modern* English judges are less political than

[52] Atiyah, note 50 above, at vi–vii. See also id. at 454.

[53] See, for example, Markesinis and Deakin, note 23 above, at 22–35.

[54] See, for example, Posner, note 12 above, esp. pts. 1 and 2. The idea was first adumbrated by Ronald Coase, in his canvass of English nuisance cases in 'The Problem of Social Cost' 3 *Journal of Law and Economics* 1 (1960). A milder version of the thesis is that economic intuitions have been highly influential in the formulation and application of common law principles. For a striking early example (for which I am indebted to A. W. Brian Simpson), see *Jones v. Powell* (1629), reprinted in J. H. Baker and S. F. C. Milsom, *Sources of English Legal History: Private Law to 1750* 601–605 (1986).

American judges. The common law of contracts was created very largely by English judges in the nineteenth century, a period in which such judges were more 'creative', or if you will political, than they are today and in which the regnant ideology was that of laissez-faire. Because modern English judges leave big changes in the law to Parliament, the wave of 'liberal' (in the sense of welfarist or egalitarian) reform that swept the Western world in the 1960s and 1970s largely bypassed the English common law of contracts, which is to say the part of that law that is in the hands of the judges. At the same time, American judges, less inclined to leave law reform to legislation, were modifying the American common law of contracts, albeit only slightly, to reflect liberal sentiment.[55]

Intuition is far from being an infallible guide to economic decision-making. Those 'liberal' American contract decisions may well have hurt rather than helped their intended beneficiaries; if creditors find it more costly to enforce defaults, or landlords to evict tenants, the cost of credit, and of rental housing, will rise, and the effect will be that of a regressive tax. The dangers of intuitive jurisprudence are well illustrated by the history of American antitrust law, a body of law that has frequently run aground on the shoals of metaphor ('leverage', 'predation', 'foreclosure', etc.). I think the English judges have stumbled occasionally in modern tort cases and could regain their balance with the help of economics. They seem to do very well with contracts, though I have suggested that economic analysis could have been pushed further in *Ruxley*, and though Atiyah has given examples—worth dwelling on briefly because they pick up a theme that I sounded in discussing the extent of liability in tort—of the inefficient application of the principle of *Hadley* v. *Baxendale*,[56] that landmark in the evolution of an economically efficient common law of contracts.

A carrier had undertaken to transport a mill shaft for repairs. As a result of the carrier's delay, which was a breach of the contract of carriage, the mill was out of service for longer than

---

[55] An example is Judge J. Skelly Wright's opinion in *Williams* v. *Walker-Thomas Furniture Co.*, 350 F.2d 445 (D.C. Cir. 1965), refusing to enforce harsh terms in credit contracts with poor borrowers.
[56] 9 Ex. 341, 156 Eng. Rep. 145 (1854).

anticipated. The owner sued for his lost profits. The carrier won the suit, rightly so from an economic standpoint. The carrier was in no position to calculate the profits of its customer's business and therefore to determine the amount of care that it would be cost-justified to take to avert their diminution. The customer might have been able to avoid the consequences of the delay, at lower cost than the carrier, simply by having a spare mill shaft. Or, if not, the customer could have offered a premium for timely service. This would have been a signal that the carrier should make a greater effort (presumably at higher cost) than it usually would to avoid delay.

The argument for excusing the contractual promisor from liability for the unforeseeable consequences of its breach is actually stronger than the parallel argument, discussed in the first part of this lecture, for excusing the tortfeasor. The tortfeasor could avoid the consequences just by doing what we want him to do anyway, which is to take due care. But breach of contract, unlike most torts, is a matter of strict liability. The promisor is not excused just because the breach was involuntary, as it often will be. Extravagant liability, because it cannot be dependably avoided by taking due care, may therefore cause promisors to take excessive care, as in the case, plausibly *Hadley* itself, in which the promisee could avoid the consequences of a breach at lower cost than the promisor and should therefore be induced to do so.

Unfortunately, the criterion of 'unforeseeability' is vague, and indeed misleading. There is very little that is unforeseeable, and Atiyah gives convincing examples of English cases in which an excessively literal interpretation of the criterion has resulted in an improper award of damages.[57] In *The Heron II*[58] for example, another case of delay by a carrier, just like *Hadley* itself, the consequence of the delay, for which the carrier was held liable, was a fall in the market price of the goods (sugar) that were being shipped. It is of course foreseeable that the market price of sugar may change between the time of shipment and the time of arrival. But it will normally be much easier and cheaper for the shipper to protect himself against the change by means of a

[57] Atiyah, note 50 above, at 480–484.
[58] *Koufos* v. *C. Czarnikow Ltd* [1969] 1 A.C. 350 (H.L. 1967).

futures contract than for the carrier to do so by any means. Moreover, price can fluctuate up as well as down. If the price had risen, the shipper would have been better off. Since the carrier could not have claimed damages on the ground that his breach made the victim of the breach better off, the rule of *The Heron II* systematically overcompensates shippers. Perhaps, with the growing diffusion of economic analysis of law throughout English contract law, *The Heron II* would be decided differently if it arose today. One cannot be completely confident of this, however, in view of cases such as *Bates* v. *Barrow Ltd* in which 'foreseeability' is understood strictly as a matter of probability.[59]

I do not want to end my discussion of modern English contract law on a negative note, so let me close with an example of impressive performance in the difficult and fascinating case of *de Balkany* v. *Christie Manson & Woods Ltd*,[60] which has attracted much attention in the art world. The plaintiff bought from the defendant, Christie's, the auction house, for a price in excess of £500,000, a painting described in the Christie's catalogue as having been painted by the well-known Austrian artist Egon Schiele. It turned out that Schiele had indeed painted and initialed the canvas but that someone had painted over Schiele's painting, covering 94 per cent of it (so that only 6 per cent of the visible surface was Schiele's work) and, in an apparent effort to pass off the overpainting as a genuine Schiele, had painted on Schiele's initials, the original initials having been effaced by the overpainting. When this was discovered, the plaintiff sought to rescind the purchase. Christie's refused, precipitating the lawsuit. The contract with the plaintiff entitled her to rescind if the painting was a 'forgery', defined as a work 'made or substantially made with an intention to deceive as to authorship . . ., which is not shown to be such in the description in the

---

[59] [1995] 1 Lloyd's Rep. 680 (Q.B. 1994). A recent case similar to *The Heron II* and reaching the same result is *The Baleares (Geogas S.A.* v. *Trammo Gas Ltd)* [1993] 1 Lloyd's Rep. 215 (C.A. 1992). Much better is *Seven Seas Properties Ltd* v. *Al-Essa* [1993] All E.R. 577 (Ch. 1992), holding that a promisor is not liable for damages arising out of the plaintiff's special susceptibility to harm unless the promisor had an opportunity to make an informed decision as to whether or not to accept the risk of that liability.

[60] Published in *The Independent*, 19 Jan. 1995, p. 8 (Q.B.).

catalogue',[61] unless 'the catalogue description was in accordance with the then generally accepted opinion of scholars'.

Against the inference of forgery Christie's pointed out that the overpainter had tried to reproduce the original composition (including colors) of Schiele's painting. Christie's argued that in effect the unknown overpainter had been trying to restore Schiele's original painting, which may have deteriorated. The painting had been made by Schiele in 1907. The overpainting had occurred sometime between 1918 and 1968. Many old (and not so old) paintings are extensively restored—and sometimes this requires some overpainting ('retouching') as well as the more usual removing of overpaint and cleaning—without being deemed forgeries. The judge rejected this argument primarily on the basis of the forged initials, which he thought showed that the overpainter had intended to deceive as to authorship. The judge pointed out that if the overpainter had either left the original initials alone or had simply strengthened them with additional brush strokes, the overpainting would have been apparent to the trained observer. So, unlike a restorer, the overpainter was trying to conceal what he had done—not surprisingly, in view of the fact that he had overpainted virtually the entire painting.

The judge's analysis is persuasive, but it could have been made even more so by the addition of a market test of forgery. A restored painting will command a higher, not a lower, price in the market than an unrestored one of equivalent quality, because a buyer of the unrestored painting would want to restore it and to do so would have to incur additional cost. A forgery of a famous artist, however, is bound to be worth much less than the genuine article, and elsewhere in his opinion the judge remarks that the painting would have been worth only £40,000—only 8 per cent of the sale price—if its true condition had been known.[62] This was additional support for deeming the

---

[61] And would have been worth much less if the deception had been known; but the satisfaction of this condition for rescission was not questioned.

[62] A loose end, however, is the judge's omission to discuss the possibility that the overpaint could have been removed and the original Schiele thus restored. In that event the painting would be worth more than £40,000, would in fact be worth £500,000 minus the cost of restoration.

painting a forgery, and it would also have been additional rebuttal to Christie's alternative defense that the overpainting had merely affected the *condition* of the painting. All Christie's paintings are sold 'as is', with full opportunity for potential buyers to inspect before the auction. The condition of a painting, as ordinarily understood, refers to physical quality—a painting is 'in good condition' if it has not deteriorated—rather than to its authenticity.

One could debate endlessly the question whether the painting was 'really' a Schiele or 'really' not. Reference to market price brings the debate down from the metaphysical to the practical level, where cases should be decided.

The judge interpreted the 'unless' clause (unless 'the catalogue description was in accordance with the then generally accepted opinion of scholars') sensibly to mean that Christie's was not responsible for the plaintiff's mistake in buying a forgery unless it was at fault (as the judge found, so that the plaintiff won) in describing the painting in its catalogue as being by Egon Schiele. At first glance one might think that, wholly apart from issues of fault, Christie's was the 'cheaper cost avoider' of the disaster that befell the plaintiff, both in the sense of being able to discover the forgery at lower cost than she and in the sense of being the superior risk bearer (insurer), able to spread the loss across its entire business, whereas the plaintiff was an individual, though doubtless a wealthy one. The contract, however, clearly disclaimed any such warranty. With that disclaimer the court's interest in who was the cheaper cost avoider was at an end. The economist might go on to observe that had Christie's given such a warranty it would have had to charge an even larger sales commission (it charged 10 per cent of the sales price). Its customers, wealthy people normally advised by their own experts, might not want to pay the extra price. They might be able to protect themselves against the risk and cost of forgery as cheaply as Christie's or even more so.

Mr. Justice Morison's opinion in *de Balkany* is very finely written (or rather, I suppose, spoken); it reaches the correct result, so far as I am able to judge; and although it could have been dressed up with some economics, it is quite adequate as is. I do not think that America has a great deal of practical value to teach English courts about contracts.

III. A NOTE ON REMEDIES

I want to examine, in closing, an interesting case of damages for securities fraud, damages in general—remedies in general— being one of the areas in which economics has had the greatest influence on American law.[63] The case is *Smith New Court Securities Ltd* v. *Scrimgeour Vickers (Asset Management) Ltd*[64] and let me give a simplified version. An investor is induced by a misrepresentation by a seller to buy shares in a company that are traded on an exchange. He pays, let us say, $50 a share and had it not been for the misrepresentation the market price would have been only $40. Some time later, but before trial, the market discovers that for reasons wholly unrelated to the misrepresentation, the shares were greatly overvalued when the plaintiff bought them. Had these reasons been known at the time, the shares would have been worth only $20 and that is the level to which they plummet when the reasons emerge. Should the plaintiff be entitled to $30 (times the number of shares he bought) in damages, the difference between what he paid as a result of the misrepresentation and the 'true' value of the shares? Or just $10, the difference between what the market price would have been on the date he purchased the shares had it not been for the misrepresentation, and the actual market price on that date? The Court of Appeal held that the latter was the proper measure of damages. The reason it gave—that the market should not be assumed 'omniscient'—is not very perspicuous, but the result is clearly correct, even assuming that if the misrepresentation had not been made the plaintiff would not have been interested in buying the stock and thus would have been spared the consequences of the plunge in the value to $20. The effect of giving the plaintiff greater damages would be to make the defendant an insurer of market fluctuations that are due to circumstances wholly beyond his control, and it is very unlikely, for reasons that the economic analysis of contracts has

---

[63] Donald Harris, *Remedies in Contract and Tort* (1988), employs economic concepts extensively to illuminate English remedies law. Harris's book has more economics than any other English legal text that I have seen.
[64] [1994] 4 All E.R. 225 (A.C.).

addressed in considerable detail, that the implicit contract between the parties included such insurance.[65] So this is a case that the English court got exactly right but that the court could have explained better with the aid of economic analysis.

[65] See my opinion in *Bastian* v. *Petren Resources Corp.*, 892 F.2d 680 (7th Cir. 1990).

Lecture Three: Functional, Systemic Comparisons of Legal Systems

I. COMPARING SYSTEMS

The contrast between this lecture and the immediately preceding one is very sharp; the difference between the two titles is a clue. Lecture Two was a romp through judicial opinions, illustrating two conventional forms of comparative legal scholarship: the comparison of doctrines, and the comparison of legal cultures as revealed in judicial opinions or other facets of judicial performance. I drew on economics but the materials that I was analyzing with the aid of economics were of a kind thoroughly familiar to lawyers.

The focus of this lecture is different. It is on comparing two operating legal systems, the English and American. By 'system' I mean a set of interrelated, interacting parts, each of which has a function in making the system work. The system itself, moreover, has a function. So system and functionality are related concepts. I emphasized functionality in Lecture One when I redefined the English 'judge' to include the barristers and the American 'judge' to include law clerks, thus substituting a functional for a formal definition of the word 'judge'. Failure to consider the operating level of a legal system is a traditional shortcoming of legal scholarship. In the area of comparative law its most lamentable manifestation was the acceptance of 'socialist law'—the phoney legal systems of the Soviet empire before its collapse—at face value. Interest in systemic interactions is traditional in economics and is one of the strengths that economics brings to the study of social system.[1]

---

[1] Ronald H. Coase, 'Economics and Contiguous Disciplines' 7 *Journal of Legal Studies* 201, 209 (1978).

The parts of a legal system are not merely institutional and procedural in character. Legal doctrines are parts of an operating legal system and they interact with the non-doctrinal parts as well as with other doctrines. A familiar Anglo-American example is the relation between the rules of evidence, which are a body of legal doctrine, and the jury, which is an institution. That is an obvious example but an important value of systemic comparison is that it can bring to light relations that are easily overlooked. Consider the much greater importance of jurisprudence as a field of teaching and study in England than in the United States. This may be connected with the fact that law in England is an undergraduate subject. The American law student is assumed to have completed his humanistic education when he received his undergraduate degree and to be ready upon entering law school to immerse himself in a technical field. That assumption would be misplaced in the case of an English law student. As a result there is a felt need to teach law in part at least as a humanity. This is done by giving the student a healthy dose of jurisprudence, a field in which the study of law is seen as continuous with the study of philosophy.

I am going to use the method of functional, systemic comparison to argue that piecemeal reform of a legal system, specifically the English legal system, is very risky and that a full comparison of the English and American legal systems, or of any two legal systems, requires the use of techniques unfamiliar to lawyers. I shall try to use those techniques both to measure and to explain some of the differences between our two systems. I shall close by offering some conjectures about the bearing of legal culture on the differences that the analysis in all three lectures has discerned between English and American law.

II. THE DANGERS OF PIECEMEAL REFORM

The *Economist* is as very intelligent news magazine. Head and shoulders above its American counterparts, it publishes competent articles about technical subjects such as the economics of human capital. Lately it has taken to advocating the reform of the English legal system.[2] Two specific changes that it advocates are abrogating the rule forbidding contingent-fee contracts[3] and abrogating the 'loser-pays' rule (the losing party to a lawsuit must reimburse the winner for the winner's reasonable expenses of suit, including attorney's fees). These rules, the *Economist* argues, limit the access to the courts of persons who have legal claims, or, more neutrally stated, make it less attractive to file civil lawsuits. This is clearly true of the ban on contingent fees. Whether it is true of the loser-pays rule is less certain. The rule makes weak cases less attractive to bring but strong cases less attractive to defend against. The net number of claims may not fall. There is even some reason, though it is far from conclusive, to think that the *settlement* rate will fall, meaning that more claims will be tried, so that judicial workloads will actually be higher than under the American rule. Legal disputants rarely go to trial, rather than settle (perhaps before even filing suit), unless both think they have a good chance of winning—that is, unless both are optimistic about the outcome of a trial. If both are pessimistic, then since a trial is more costly than a settlement they will be desperate to settle. In a loser-pays regime, the optimists will be optimistic about recovering their fees (which would not happen with a settlement), and this will give them an additional incentive to sue. As we shall see, however, this effect may be offset by the tendency of the loser-pays rule to make litigation more costly.[4]

---

[2] See 'Bring the Balance Back' *Economist*, 14 Jan. 1995, p. 13; 'Civil Justice in Britain: Trial and Error: Using the Civil Courts in Britain Is Now Too Expensive and Too Risky for All But the Very Poor and the Very Wealthy' id., p. 29; 'Britain's Antiquated Courts: They Are Excluding Too Many People and Costing the Taxpayer a Fortune' *Economist*, 16 Sept. 1995, p. 20.

[3] A proposed change that has already been partially implemented, as I noted in Lecture One, in accordance with a proposal in a noted 'green paper' issued by the Lord Chancellor. Lord Chancellor's Department, 'Contingency Fees' (Her Majesty's Stationery Office, Cm 571, Jan. 1989).

[4] Economic analysis of the loser-pays rule is extensive. See, for example, Richard A. Posner, *Economic Analysis of Law* 570–574 (4th ed. 1992); Steven Shavell, 'Suit, Settlement, and Trial: A Theoretical Analysis under Alternative Methods for the Allocation of Legal Costs' 11 *Journal of Legal Studies* 55 (1982); James W. Hughes and Edward A. Snyder, 'Litigation and Settlement under the English and American Rules: Theory and Evidence' 38 *Journal of Law and Economics* 225, 227–228 (1995); John C. Hause, 'Indemnity, Settlement, and Litigation, or I'll Be Suing You' 18 *Journal of Legal Studies* 157 (1989).

I want to set these details to one side for now and simply point out that the *Economist* has overlooked the fact that both rules, the loser-pays rule and the ban (now quasi-ban) on contingent-fee contracts, are functioning parts of a system and that you should not change a functioning part before examining the effect of the change on the operation of the system. It would be foolish to suggest installing an airplane battery in an automobile on the ground that airplane batteries are more reliable; the airplane battery would not fit. The English and American legal systems are like the automobile and the airplane. Contingent fees and winner-bears-his-own-legal-expenses are features of the American system that the *Economist* thinks the English system should borrow. It does not consider whether they would fit that system. We saw in Lecture One that the loser-pays rule and the ban on contingent fees serve, along with other features of the English legal system, the purpose of inducing barristers to perform judicial functions, enabling England to get by with a tiny number of official judges. England would need many more official judges if barristers operated under the same incentives and constraints as American lawyers. Before advocating the abrogation of the two rules the *Economist* should have considered the feasibility and desirability of multiplying the number of English judges, equipping them with law clerks, or, in general, restructuring the English judiciary along American lines.

The two rules interact not only with other parts of the English legal system but also with each other. Without contingent fees it is difficult for individuals and small firms to finance civil litigation. The loser-pays rule provides a partial substitute. It facilitates the bringing at least of strong cases, because in such cases the lawyer for the plaintiff has a reasonable probability of being paid his fee by the defendant, so that the lawyer's fee will not eat into the plaintiff's winnings. But if contingent-fee contracts are permitted yet the loser-pays rule is retained, litigation may explode. For as I just noted, the loser-pays rule may increase the rate of litigation, and so may multiply the effect of contingent-fee financing of litigation. It is not surprising that most of the world's legal systems have both the loser-pays rule *and* a rule against contingent fees.

I have a similar reservation about the elimination of the

barristers' monopoly of appearing in the higher courts. That the barristers defend their privileged position by reference to the public interest even though their principal motives are doubtless financial (or so Adam Smith would have thought, not to mention Dickens) and that barristers' actual performance falls short of the quasi-judicial ideal sketched in Lecture One[5] do not change the fact that making them more like American lawyers would require major changes in the staffing and practices of the English judiciary.

The underlying reason that proposals to deregulate the English bar are superficial is that competition has a dual significance in the market for legal services. On the one hand, it conduces to better service to clients. On the other hand, it increases the cost to the lawyer of subordinating his client's interest to that of justice, or the judiciary, or even just his own interest in becoming a judge or a QC. If the remaining barriers to competition in the English legal profession are dismantled, we can expect that, just as has happened in the United States in recent years with the growth of competition in the legal profession, lawyers will become better agents of their clients and worse agents of the courts. The fewer official judges a legal system has, the less it can afford to have lawyers who owe sole allegiance to their clients.

I must not commit the same mistake as the *Economist* and make suggestions for change without considering their system-wide impact. I urged in Lecture Two a greater attention to economics by English judges. I must consider how this might affect other parts of the English legal system. No doubt it would require some changes in legal education, not only in the content of courses but also in the selection of law teachers. If one may judge by the American experience, the necessary changes would not be large. The more troublesome question is whether judicial performance would suffer in some dimension if judges

[5] Robert J. Martineau, *Appellate Justice in England and the United States: A Comparative Analysis* 123–127 (1990). But Martineau's point, which is supported by my own limited exposure to English appellate advocacy, is not that the barristers are not trustworthy, but that they are not very impressive advocates. The points may be related. The barrister's effort to serve the court may reduce the polemical vigor and thrust of his arguments.

became more receptive to economic arguments and evidence. This concern is expressed frequently in the United States by critics of the law and economics movement. I do not consider it well founded. The American judges who have brought economic perspectives or intuitions to their decision-making are, in general, highly regarded.[6] They include Holmes, Brandeis, Hand, and the numerous 'law and economics' alumni who have become federal appellate judges in recent years. The reason economics can be worked into legal analysis without changing the fundamental character of that analysis is the isomorphism of economic and legal thought. Much economic analysis of law in the United States has consisted of showing how judges and other formulators or designers of legal doctrines and institutions have used intuition to arrive at results that are at least broadly consistent with economic efficiency.[7] Indeed, this was a theme of Lecture Two.

Another piecemeal reform of the Ensglish legal system also seems feasible, indeed inevitable, though not wholly without peril. The fetish of 'orality', which greatly impairs the productivity of English judges and causes enormous inconvenience to lawyers and litigants,[8] is eroding rapidly[9]—particularly in the criminal courts, where most appeals are now decided on the papers (the application for leave to appeal and the response to it)—without a substantial adverse effect, so far as I am able to judge, on the functioning of the legal system. Oral argument and oral evidence, even oral judicial opinions, are valuable components of a judicial process, but they can be overdone. England can no longer cope with its appellate caseload without limiting the length of oral argument.[10] Largely, it seems, because English appellate judges spend so much time listening to argument, in 1986 the average number of appeals decided, per appellate judge, was only 38.1, compared to 118.5 in the federal courts of appeals.[11] My own experience as a judge has persuaded me that

---

[6] I realize that this is an absurdly self-serving statement.

[7] See *Economic Analysis of Law*, note 4 above.

[8] Martineau, note 5 above, ch. 3; Patrick Devlin, *The Judge* 59 (1979).

[9] See, for example, Martineau, note 5 above, at 245–248. The cause is undoubtedly the pressure of a rapidly growing caseload. See Part IV of this lecture.   [10] Martineau, note 5 above, at 247–248.

[11] Id. at 161–162; the U.S. figure is for 1987.

very few cases benefit from more than 20 minutes of oral argument per side. And, having likened barristers to law clerks, let me point out that law clerks generally communicate with their judges more in writing (in the form of memoranda and opinion drafts) than orally.

There is, however, a greater downside in the curtailment of oral argument by English courts than by American ones. The shorter oral argument is, the less give and take is possible between judges and counsel, and the less perfectly therefore the barrister can play the role of law clerk. We recall from Lecture One Lord Woolf's proposal to curtail oral argument *and* hire law clerks.

The proposals are linked in another way. The pressure to limit oral argument comes mainly from the growth of the caseload, and that growth is also a reason for hiring law clerks in order to increase the productive capacity of the judiciary without expanding the number of judges. But combining a reduction in oral argument with the hiring of law clerks cannot be the complete answer to caseload pressures for England, as it may be for the United States. We recall from Lecture One the un-representative character of the English judiciary, its lack of political legitimacy. One response, we saw, was positivism. Another is orality. When everything is done in the open—when there are no briefs, when the judges do no private research and have no staffs, and when they do not even deliberate at the end of an argument but immediately deliver their opinions seriatim—public monitoring of judicial performance is facilitated. The judges can be *seen* to be doing, or not doing, justice. This was the traditional defense of orality.[12] If through law clerks and briefs and reserved decisions and private deliberations the judges bring a large part of the judicial process behind the scenes, the public may demand substitute means for assuring accountability. The explicitly bureaucratic (disciplined, monitored) structure of the Continental judiciaries can thus be seen as one substitute for the English tradition of judicial orality,

[12] See, for example, Devlin, note 8 above, at 58; Jack I. H. Jacob, *The Fabric of English Civil Justice* 19–23 (1987). Chancery proceedings, originally 'paper' proceedings though less so today, remain a limited exception to the principle of orality. Id. at 21.

and the American system of politically legitimated judges (through election or senatorial confirmation) as another.

III. WHICH SYSTEM IS BETTER?

The largest question presented by the *Economist*'s criticisms of the English legal system is whether the American system is better. The American system is, of course, widely derided—today more than ever. But much of the derision is based on unreliable (sometimes outright false) anecdotes or isolated cases. The *Economist* rightly warns against basing an evaluation of a system that processes many millions of cases a year on a few headline-grabbing anomalies.[13] How then is one to make a comparative evaluation of the systems? My answer is: with data.

A. *The Cost of Litigation*

Critics of the English system argue that it is very expensive to litigate a case in England and that as a result many meritorious suits are never brought. It is difficult to obtain good data on the cost of litigation in either country, in part because of the extreme heterogeneity of lawsuits. So it is hard to say whether litigation really is more costly in England than in the United States. My impression is that it probably costs about the same in the two countries to litigate similar cases. English courts, however, are less generous than American ones in awarding damages. This is partly because of doctrinal differences, some discussed in

---

[13] 'The Way Those Crazy Americans Do It' *Economist*, 14 Jan. 1995, p. 31. Inconsistently, the *Economist* uses anecdote to bolster its case for reform, pointing for example to a suit between neighbors over a few square feet of disputed land in which the losing party was ordered to pay the winner £85,000 in legal expenses—more than half the value of the loser's property. 'Justice in Britain' note 2 above, p. 29. The point of the anecdote is unclear. The loser put the winner to the expense of defending against an unmeritorious suit, so it does not seem so unreasonable that the loser should be made to pay. Apparently the *Economist*'s point (blurred by its advocacy of abrogating the loser-pays rule) is that it should not have cost so much to litigate a dispute in which the stakes were so low. My own view is that if two people want to squander their resources on spite litigation, they should be allowed to do so, provided they bear the full costs of the litigation, including the costs to the judiciary itself.

Lecture Two, such as the much greater difficulty of obtaining an award of punitive damages in an English court; partly because juries are almost never used in English civil cases; and partly because incomes are lower in England[14] and lost earnings are a big component of damages in many tort and employment cases. For these reasons, the ratio of expense to recovery is, it appears, higher in England than in the United States. Legal expenses have been estimated to equal 50 to 75 per cent of damages in High Court cases, which is not so out of line with the corresponding American figures,[15] but to equal 125 per cent in cases tried in the county courts,[16] where most civil cases are tried.[17] These figures imply that the net expected gain from suit in an English court is likely to be small unless the claim is for a very large amount and is likely to succeed. It is not that it is more expensive to litigate a claim in England than in America but that it is less worthwhile to do so because the expected recovery net of legal expenses is smaller.

It might seem that an offsetting factor would be the generous scale of civil legal aid in England. In 1994 it amounted to some £590 million net of receipts,[18] the equivalent of about

[14] The U.K. Gross Domestic Product per capita is 74.3 per cent of the U.S. as measured by exchange rates, and 73.8 per cent as measured by purchasing power. *Human Development Report 1994* 184 (United Nations Development Programme 1994) (tab. 28) (1991 figures).

[15] James S. Kakalik and Nicholas M. Pace, *Costs and Compensation Paid in Tort Litigation* (RAND Institute for Civil Justice R-3391-ICJ 1986).

[16] These figures are from Report to Parliament by the Lord Chancellor, *Civil Justice Review: Report of the Review Body on Civil Justice* 80 (Her Majesty's Stationery Office, Cm 394, June 1988). The data are from the early 1980s.

[17] Other surveys are consistent. See studies summarized in Timothy M. Swanson, 'The Importance of Contingency Fee Agreements' 11 *Oxford Journal of Legal Studies* 193, 195–200 (1991); Lord Woolf, *Access to Justice: Interim Report to the Lord Chancellor on the Civil Justice System in England and Wales* 10, 251–260 (June 1995). For example, in 32 per cent of the cases analyzed in Lord Woolf's report, the allowed costs, which is to say the legal expenses of the winning party alone, exceeded 50 per cent of the value of the claim. Id. at 256. Filing fees are also higher in English courts. For example, the fee for filing a case in the High Court is £120 (roughly $192), compared to $120 for filing a case in a U.S. district court. For an interesting discussion of Lord Woolf's report, see Richard L. Marcus,' "*Déjà Vu* All Over Again?" An American Reaction to the Woolf Report' in *Reform of Civil Procedure: Essays on 'Access to Justice'* 219 (A. A. S. Zuckerman and Ross Cranston eds. 1995).

[18] Computed from Lord Chancellor's Department, *Judicial Statistics, England and Wales, for the Year 1994* 102 (Her Majesty's Stationery Office, Cm 2891, July 1995).

$900 million. This is more than twice the appropriation for the Legal Services Corporation, the federal dispenser of civil legal aid funds in the United States.[19] There is very little non-federal public civil legal aid. There is some charitable support and some donation of private lawyers' time (*pro bono* practice, as it is called), as is true in England as well,[20] though presumably on a much smaller scale than in the United States, but I have no figures. The *Economist* contends that civil legal aid is dispensed very wastefully, so that the poor and near-poor are badly served.[21] I cannot evaluate this contention. But as people who are not poor usually cannot qualify for legal aid, it is not an adequate substitute for the contingent fee as a method of financing litigation by a middle-class plaintiff. Most accident victims, the commonest type of potential civil plaintiff, are neither wealthy nor poor.

Analysis is further complicated by the loser-pays rule. Under that rule, if a plaintiff has a solid case, the expense of litigating falls out of the picture; he will recover that expense when he wins. Although the rule may seem a fearsome deterrent to plaintiffs who do not have an airtight case, it seems that only about 40 per cent of English plaintiffs are subject, as a practical matter, to having to pay the defendant's legal expenses if the defendant wins. The rest are legal-aid clients, are funded by their union, or carry legal insurance.[22] Nor would I expect the fact that a barrister cannot be expected to fight for his client's cause with all the bareknuckled enthusiasm of the typical

---

[19] See generally Marianne Wilder Young, 'The Need for Legal Aid Reform: A Comparison of English and American Legal Aid' 24 *Cornell International Law Journal* 379 (1991) (student note).

[20] Alan Paterson, 'Financing Legal Services: A Comparative Perspective' in *The Option of Litigating in Europe* 149, 150 (D. L. Carey Miller and Paul R. Beaumont eds. 1993).

[21] 'Justice in Britain' note 2 above.

[22] Herbert M. Kritzer, 'The English Experience with the English Rule: How "Loser Pays" Works, What Difference It Makes, and What Might Happen Here' 4–6 (University of Wisconsin-Madison, Institute for Legal Studies, Disputes Processing Research Program, Working Paper DPRP 11–4, July 1992). However, the percentage of tort claimants who are subject to having to pay the defendant's legal expenses if the defendant wins is higher, and apparently many of them either abandon their claims or accept very low offers in settlement. Id. at 7.

American trial lawyer[23] to affect the chances of a plaintiff succeeding in an English court. Just as with the loser-pays rule, there is an offsetting effect: the defendant's barrister will fight less hard. It is the absence of contingent fees that puts the biggest damper on the filing of claims (especially tort claims, since most tort claimants are individuals of modest means), because it prevents claimants from borrowing the expenses of suit from a lawyer. The financing aspect of contingent-fee contracts is important and probably dominates their effect both in screening out marginal suits (see Lecture One) and in reducing litigation in the long run through deterring negligent and other tortious behavior by increasing the likelihood of suit.[24]

Since average earnings are lower in England than in the United States and since lawyers' fees are the principal expense of litigation, it might seem that if I am right that the cost of litigation is about the same in the two countries this must be because the English legal profession is more monopolistic than the American. Perhaps. But an alternative possibility is that the loser-pays rule induces greater expenditure per litigation. Recall that rational disputants will settle their dispute unless both expect to do better in litigation than in settlement. The more optimistic each one is about winning, the less costly (under the loser-pays rule) will additional expenditures on trying to win seem, and also the greater will be the expected benefit of seeking to influence the outcome by an additional expenditure.[25]

B. *The Relative Sizes of the Systems*

With all factors considered it is merely a guess that the incentive to sue is weaker in England than in the United States. But it is a

---

[23] This is not because of the loser-pays rule. If anything, that should increase the incentive of the barrister to fight hard, by increasing the net expected payoff from suit. The reason that barristers can be expected not to fight so hard as American trial lawyers is the barrister's role as a judicial adjunct, which I discussed in Lecture One.

[24] This second effect is discussed in Thomas J. Miceli and Kathleen Segerson, 'Contingent Fees for Lawyers: The Impact on Litigation and Accident Prevention' 20 *Journal of Legal Studies* 381 (1991), and in Neil Rickman, 'The Economics of Contingency Fees in Personal Injury Litigation' 10 *Oxford Review of Economic Policy* 34, 47 (1994).   [25] Hughes and Snyder, note 4 above, at 227.

guess supported, although weakly, by the disproportionately smaller scale of the English legal system. The qualifier 'disproportionately' is vital. Since the population of England is only 20 per cent that of the United States,[26] one cannot expect it to have so large a legal system. I shall assume therefore that England's legal system is smaller than the U.S. legal system only if it is less than 20 per cent the size of the U.S. system. This method of commensurating the two systems is extremely crude. There is no clear-cut relation between population and legal activity any more than there is between per capita income and legal activity—one effect of a growing value of time being to make litigation, a highly time-intensive activity, disproportionately more expensive. A larger population will increase the universe of potential legal disputes by increasing the number of interactions, some bound to cause injury, among persons. But the propensity to litigate depends critically (and this wholly apart from 'litigiousness') on the number of legal rights, the cost of enforcing them, and the law's uncertainty—factors likely to swamp differences in population. Over the century ending in 1960 there was very little growth in federal litigation in the United States (except for a blip during Prohibition) despite enormous growth in both population and per capita income, while since 1960 there has been enormous growth in federal litigation despite a slowing of the rate of population and economic growth.[27] Still, the difference in population between England and America is so great that it is reasonable to expect the English legal system to be significantly smaller than the American.

It is even smaller than expected. We know from Lecture One that the number of English lawyers is not 20 per cent of the American number but only 10 per cent. International comparisons of numbers of lawyers are often derided by pointing

---

[26] By 'England' I mean, as noted in the Preface, England and Wales, which have a population of about 51 million, compared to about 255 million in the United States.

[27] See Richard A. Posner, *The Federal Courts: Challenge and Reform*, ch. 3 (Harvard University Press, forthcoming, 1996), for detailed statistics. Between 1904, the first year for which statistics on the number of cases filed in the federal district courts are available, and 1960, the annual compound rate of increase in the number of cases filed annually was only 1.8 per cent.

out that tasks performed in one country by lawyers may be performed in another by people who are called something else.[28] My insistence on functionally reclassifying barristers as judges makes me sympathetic to this kind of criticism. But I do not think it warrants an assumption that the English legal system, relative to the American, is bigger than it looks. My guess is that as high a proportion of legal services are supplied in America by people who are not called lawyers, but instead are called paralegals, tax preparers, union grievers, lay advocates ('jailhouse lawyers'), law students, ombudsmen, and trust officers, as is true of England. It is only a guess because at least through the 1970s England had a higher ratio of paralegals (called 'legal executives') to lawyers than the United States did.[29]

Let me turn from number of lawyers to number of cases, beginning with appeals. The total number of appeals filed with all the English appellate tribunals (Privy Council, House of Lords, Court of Appeal, and High Court,[30] was 13,562 in 1994.[31] In the U.S. federal courts alone, the corresponding figure was almost four times as great.[32] The federal courts are only a small part of the American judiciary. There are more than 30 times as many state as federal judges,[33] and state judges tend to have heavier caseloads than federal judges. When the number of

[28] For an excellent discussion, see Dietrich Rueschemeyer, 'Comparing Legal Professions: A State-Centered Approach' in *Lawyers in Society*, vol. 3: *Comparative Theories* 289 (Richard L. Abel and Philip S. C. Lewis eds. 1989).

[29] Quintin Johnstone and John A. Flood, in their article 'Paralegals in English and American Law Offices' 2 *Windsor Yearbook of Access to Justice* 152, 155, 174 (1982), estimate the number of American paralegals in the 1970s as 30,000–80,000 and the number of English paralegals as 20,000. By 1992 there were 95,000 paralegals in the United States. American Bar Association Commission on Nonlawyer Practice, *Nonlawyer Activity in Law-Related Situations: A Report with Recommendations* 51 (Aug. 1995). I have not been able to find a current figure for England.

[30] The High Court has both trial and appellate jurisdiction. See Appendix A at the end of this book.

[31] *Judicial Statistics, England and Wales, for the Year 1994*, note 18 above, at 17 (tab. 1.17).

[32] Posner, note 27 above, is the source for all my federal-court statistics. The basic statistics are in id., ch. 3, esp. tabs. 3.1–3.3.

[33] Compare Brian J. Ostrom et al., *State Court Caseload Statistics: Annual Report 1992* 9 (National Center for State Courts Feb. 1994), with Posner, note 27 above, ch. 1, tab. 1.1.

appeals to state intermediate and final appellate courts[34] is added to the number of federal appeals, the total exceeds 300,000. This exceeds the corresponding figure for England by a ratio that is closer to 25 to 1 than it is to 5 to 1.

Comparison at the trial level is extremely difficult because the jurisdiction of the county courts cuts right across the line that separates courts of general jurisdiction from courts of limited jurisdiction in the United States. The English courts that correspond most closely to American trial courts, state and federal, that have a general jurisdiction are the Chancery and Queen's Bench Divisions of the High Court, and the Crown Court, where all trials on indictment are prosecuted. In 1994, 167,221 civil cases, excluding appeals and insolvency cases,[35] and 89,301 criminal cases were filed in these three courts.[36] This is about the same number of cases as were filed in the federal district courts that year, but those courts handle only a tiny fraction of the total number of cases filed in all American courts of general jurisdiction. In 1992, more than 22 million cases were filed in state courts of general jurisdiction.[37] The total number of cases filed in the county courts of England that year was 3.7 million, of which 3.4 million were 'money plaints'.[38] Although there is no recorded subject-matter breakdown of the money plaints, I am told that at least 90 per cent are summonses for non-payment of bills and are not contested.[39] If those 90 per cent are subtracted, and the cases in the Chancery and Queen's Bench Divisions and the Crown Court are added, we come up with a figure of 900,000

[34]   259,276 in 1992. Ostrom et al., note 33 above, at 50.

[35]   I exclude insolvency cases because in the United States most of them are handled by special courts of limited jurisdiction, the bankruptcy courts, a division of the federal district courts. Statistics on cases filed in the district courts exclude cases filed in the bankruptcy courts.

[36]   *Judicial Statistics, England and Wales, for the year 1994*, note 18 above, at 20 (tab. 2.1), 27, 63 (tab. 6.1). I exclude from the count of criminal cases certain non-trial matters that the Crown Court handles, see id. at 62–63, as well as the vast number of minor crimes and violations (mainly traffic offences) that are handled by magistrates—matters that correspond to the tens of millions of violations, again mostly traffic offenses, handled by American courts of limited jurisdiction.

[37]   Ostrom et al., note 33 above, at 6.

[38]   *Judicial Statistics, England and Wales, for the Year 1994*, note 18 above, at 39 (tab. 4.1).

[39]   Consistent with this estimate, the *Civil Justice Review*, note 16 above, at 111, found that 74 per cent of the money plaints in the county courts were for less than £500.

cases to compare with the more than 22 million cases filed in American courts of general jurisdiction that year—a ratio of 23:1 in favor of the American filings.

Still another measure of the difference in scale between the two systems is the difference in the number of trials. That difference, it appears, is even greater than the difference in the number of cases because English cases are less likely to be decided by a trial. In the Queen's Bench Division in 1994, the ratio of completed trials to cases filed was a minuscule .0036:1; the corresponding ratio for the civil side of the federal district courts was .0442:1, which is more than ten times greater.[40] The reason may be that since the stakes in English lawsuits are smaller on average than the stakes in American suits, yet the costs of trial appear to be comparable, the incentive to settle before incurring those costs is very great.

C. *The Performance of the Systems*

In General

These quantitative comparisons must be taken with a grain of salt. Yet even after making allowance for the difficulty of comparison, it is a good guess that England really does have a disproportionately smaller legal system than the United States, whether measured by personnel or by activity (at least litigation activity). Is this good or bad? The answer may depend on *why* the English system is disproportionately smaller. There are three plausible explanations, and they are not mutually exclusive: the expected gains from suing are less, yet suing is more difficult to finance because of the absence of the contingent fee; the English have fewer judicially enforceable rights; English law is clearer.

I have discussed the first point, but have not elucidated its normative implications. On the one hand, if meritorious suits cannot be maintained, the deterrent and other objectives of law are undermined. On the other hand, if non-meritorious suits cannot be maintained, the law's objectives are promoted.

---

[40] The sources for these computations are *Judicial Statistics, England and Wales, for the Year 1994*, note 18 above, at 29–30 (tabs. 3.1, 3.4), and Posner, note 27 above, ch. 3, tabs. 3.2, 3.3.

Probably the English system discourages both sorts of suit, but perhaps the latter disproportionately because of the loser-pays rule. This is wild speculation but I shall offer a little evidence shortly.

The English have fewer rights than Americans do not only because of the absence of a written, judicially enforceable constitution but also because the array of statutory and common law rights is much smaller.[41] Whether this is a good or a bad thing would require going right by right, law by law, through the entire *corpus juris* of the United States and England, evaluating the effects of each right, each law, on the social welfare. It is unclear what the result of that gargantuan undertaking would be. There is no doubt that the United States has many foolish, litigation-spawning statutes that England has been spared.[42] But what the overall balance would be I do not know.

The third possible explanation for England's lower level of litigation may seem an unequivocal good from the standpoint of social welfare. The clearer law is, the less room there is for legal disputes; and who, except the trial lawyers, can object to clarity in law? I pointed out earlier that unless each party to a legal dispute is optimistic about winning, a case is much more likely to be settled than to be litigated. If the law is clear, this mutual optimism is unlikely; both parties will have a realistic, rather than an optimistic, understanding of their chances.

I am fairly secure about the minor premise: English law is clearer than American. Some evidence may be found in a comparison of the ages of cited cases, shown in Table 3.1 (pages 86 and 87). In the Court of Appeal, the average age of cited decisions rendered by the House of Lords (18.62 years) is similar to that of decisions of the U.S. Supreme Court cited in federal

[41] This is in general, not in every case. English workers, unlike American workers, can bring common law suits against their employers for injuries from accidents on the job. See P. W. J. Bartrip, *Workmen's Compensation in Twentieth Century Britain: Law, History and Social Policy*, ch. 10 (1987). And English defamation law is stricter than American. I am speaking, moreover, of justiciable rights; in both countries there are alternative methods of dispute resolution or claims enforcement to the use of the courts.

[42] A notable example is the Age Discrimination in Employment Act, which has no counterpart in England. See Richard A. Posner, *Aging and Old Age*, ch. 13 (1995).

courts of appeals (19.10 years); but the average age of citations in the Court of Appeal to other courts (28.38 years) is several times higher than the corresponding figure (9.9 years) for the federal courts of appeals.[43] English cases 'turn over' less frequently than American, implying a lower rate of legal change. An alternative explanation for the greater average age of English cases is, however, simply that the pool of recent cases is smaller.

The U.S. courts of appeals and the English Court of Appeal do not have identical jurisdictions. But as shown in Table 3.2 (page 88), there is considerable overlap in areas like torts, contracts, admiralty, intellectual property, criminal law, and bankruptcy. And we can see in Table 3.1 that the higher 'other court' citations ages in the English sample are found in these subsamples as well.

Another way to get at the question of clarity is to compare appeal rates. Unfortunately, these are not reported judicial statistics but have to be constructed, and that is difficult to do because the number of appealable orders is also not a reported statistic. A very crude method of approximating appeal rates is to compare the number of cases filed with the number of appeals taken. For the federal courts in 1994 this method of estimation yields a civil appeal rate of 13.7 per cent.[44] The closest comparison that I am able to make with England is to divide the number of cases filed in the Queen's Bench Division (where most High Court civil cases are filed) in 1994, 157,453, by the number of appeals (both final and interlocutory) filed in the civil division of the Court of Appeal that year, a meager 1,683,[45] yielding an infinitesimal appeal rate of 1.1 per cent.

A better method of estimating appeal rates, which yields, incidentally, a less dramatic disparity between the two countries, is to compare the number of appeals filed with the number of cases resolved in the trial court with some court action. So estimated, the civil appeal rate in the federal courts was 17.2 per cent

---

[43] The U.S. figures are from a study of a sample of federal court of appeals cases decided in 1974 and 1975. See William M. Landes and Richard A. Posner, 'Legal Precedent: A Theoretical and Empirical Analysis' 19 *Journal of Law and Economics* 249, 256 (1976) (tab. 2). The English figures are based on a random sample of 200 Court of Appeal decisions in 1994.

[44] Posner, note 27 above, ch. 4, tab. 4.2.

[45] *Judicial Statistics, England and Wales, for the Year 1994*, note 18 above, at 17 (tab. 1.17), 29 (tab. 3.1).

Table 3.1 Average Age (In Years) of English and American Judicial Citations

Subject-matter Classification of Cases	English Court of Appeal Cases (1994) Cited Court			U.S. Courts of Appeals Cases (1974–1975) Cited Court	
	All Courts Age (weighted average)[a] [Std. Dev.]	House of Lords Age (weighted average) [No. of Citations]	Other Courts Age (weighted average) [No. of Citations]	Supreme Court Age (weighted average) [No. of Citations]	Other Courts Age (weighted average) [No. of Citations]
Common Law	26.04 [33.64]	28.9 [10]	25.8 [119]	33.8 [213]	14.8 [1061]
Torts and Contracts	25.53 [34.7]	20.5 [6]	25.81 [105]	35.6 [137]	15.7 [856]
Admiralty	29.17 [26.79]	41.5 [4]	25.65 [14]	30.6 [76]	10.9 [205]
Economic Regulation	25.43 [27.35]	6.8 [5]	27.95 [37]	19.5 [588]	10.3 [1660]
Tax	27.83 [21.35]	5 [1]	32.4 [5]	26.1 [66]	15.1 [324]
Antitrust	0 [–]	0 [0]	0 [0]	19.1 [50]	6.5 [107]
Labor	10.14 [7.24]	12 [1]	9.83 [6]	14.9 [186]	8.3 [433]

Gov. Regulatory Agencies	16.9 [18.9]	13 [1]	17.39 [8]	19.2 [240]	8.0 [510]
Patents, copyrights, and trade marks	33.9 [33.6]	2 [2]	37.44 [18]	30.7 [46]	13.2 [286]
Civil Rights	32.5 [21.92]	0 [0]	32.5 [2]	10.1 [172]	4.0 [402]
Constitutional	16.2 [8.84]	0 [0]	16.2 [5]	12.6 [136]	5.5 [155]
Criminal	17.3 [26.96]	8.83 [6]	18.01 [72]	16.2 [999]	8.0 [2056]
Bankruptcy	93.79 [108.91]	0 [0]	93.97 [14]	37.4 [14]	14.7 [155]
Military	0 [–]	0 [0]	0 [0]	11.1 [31]	6.0 [82]
Property	49.54 [46.7]	30.03 [3]	52.09 [23]	50.2 [60]	22.9 [61]
Family Law	23.09 [29.82]	9 [3]	23.89 [35]	–	–
Immigration	0.1 [0]	2 [2]	0.1 [35]	–	–
Not Classified	7 [2.77]	0 [0]	7 [7]	–	–
Total	27.65 [40.82]	18.62 [26]	28.38 [320]	19.1 [2278]	9.9 [5785]

a The average age of all the citations within the particular subject-matter class.

Table 3.2 Subject-Matter Breakdown of Court of Appeals Caseload in England and the United States

Subject-matter Classification of Cases	English Court of Appeal Cases (1994)		U.S. Courts of Appeals Cases (1974–1975)	
	No.	%	No.	%
Common Law	84	42.0	115	17.5
Torts and Contract	82	41.0	94	14.3
Admiralty	2	1.0	21	3.2
Economic Regulation	21	10.5	183	27.8
Tax	3	1.5	36	5.5
Antitrust	0	0.0	12	1.8
Labor	6	3.0	53	8.1
Gov. Regulatory Agencies	9	4.5	50	7.6
Patents, copyrights, and trade marks	3	1.5	32	4.9
Civil Rights	4	2.0	47	7.1
Constitutional	2	1.0	65	9.9
Criminal	42	21.0	239	36.3
Bankruptcy	2	1.0	17	2.6
Military	0	0.0	11	1.7
Property	8	4.0	8	1.2
Family Law	27	13.5	–	–
Immigration	7	3.5	–	–
Not Classified	3	1.5	19	2.9
Total	200		658	

in 1994.[46] The corresponding estimate for appeals from the Queen's Bench Division that year is 9.5 per cent.[47] The disparity, though smaller, is further evidence that English law is clearer than American, as is the fact that the likelihood of reversal, once an appeal is taken, is considerably higher in the

[46] Posner, note 27 above, ch. 4, tab. 4.5.
[47] Computed from *Judicial Statistics, England and Wales, for the Year 1994*, note 18 above, at 12–13 (tabs. 1.9, 1.10), 30 (tabs. 3.3, 3.4).

English Court of Appeal than in the federal courts of appeals.[48]
The inference is that only the close cases are being appealed, the
law being clear enough to discourage appeals in other cases.

The disparity in appeal rates between the two legal systems
might be even greater were it not for England's loser-pays rule,
for that rule increases the incentive to appeal. A prevailing
appellant not only obtains the benefit that an appellant in an
American court would obtain from a successful appeal—the
reversal of an adverse judgment. He also (if he goes on to win
the case) recovers his legal expenses in the trial court and
reverses the award of his opponent's expenses in that court. Of
course he risks having to pay his opponent's expenses on appeal
if the judgment of the lower court is affirmed. But if expenses on
appeal are only a small fraction of the expenses at trial, the
appellant will have more to gain from appealing than would an
American appellant who had the identical prospects for over-
turning the judgment in the lower court.[49]

The inference from Table 3.1 and from the comparison of
appeal rates is that the law administered by the U.S. courts is
more fluid and changeable than the law administered by the
English courts. This does not prove that the English legal system
is superior, however. Certainty of legal obligation, although
good, is not the only good of a legal system, and it must be
traded off against the good of adapting law to changing

---

[48] Burton Atkins, 'Interventions and Power in Judicial Hierarchies: Appellate
Courts in England and the United States,' 24 *Law and Society Review* 71, 83–87
(1990).

[49] Let P be the appellant's probability of winning the appeal, J the judgment
that he will obtain (or knock out, if he is the defendant and lost in the trial court),
C_t the legal expense that he incurred at trial (and I shall assume that his
opponent's expense was the same), and C_a the legal expense he will incur in the
appeal (likewise assumed to be equal to his opponent's expense). Under the
American rule, whereby each party bears his own legal expenses, the expected
benefit of the appeal is simply $PJ - C_a$. Under the loser-pays rule it is $P(J + C_t + C_a) -
C_a - (1 - P)C_a$. For, if the appellant wins (with probability = P), he recovers not
only the judgment but also his legal expenses in both trial and appellate court,
while if he loses (probability = $1 - P$), he is out of pocket merely his and his
opponent's legal expenses in the appellate court. If, as we know from the earlier
discussion is quite plausible, $C_t = J$, and assuming arbitrarily but not unreasonably
that C_a is only one-fifth the size of C_t and that P is .5, the expected benefit of appeal
under the American rule simplifies to $.5J - .2J = .3J$, while the expected benefit
under the English rule simplifies to $.5(J + J + .2J) - .2J - .5 (.2J) = .8J$ and is thus
larger.

circumstances. But the greater certainty of English law may well be a partial explanation for the smaller caseload of the English judicial system.

I want to consider *why* English law is more certain than American. The reasons include the homogeneity of the judiciary and of the bar, which facilitates mutual understanding and hence prediction; the absence of a judicially enforceable constitution[50] and of a federal system, institutions that create confusing duplications and inconsistencies in legal obligation; and the superior ability of a highly centralized parliamentary system to enact clear laws and keep them up to date. The strikingly low rate of growth of English caseloads, which we see in Table 3.3, is probably both an additional cause, and an effect, of legal certainty. Since 1913, the last year before World War I, the number of appeals filed has increased ninefold, the number of cases filed in the Queen's Bench Division (then King's Bench) two and a half times, and the number of cases in the county courts threefold.[51] Unfortunately there are no nationwide U.S. judicial statistics for any period before the 1980s. But statistics for just the federal courts reveal that the number of appeals in those courts has increased thirtyfold (from 1,465 in 1913 to 42,983 in 1995), while the number of first instance civil filings has increased more than fifteenfold (from 14,935 to 236,391).[52]

The modesty of English judges is also a factor in the greater certainty of English law, as is the firmer commitment of English than of American judges to the principle of stare decisis, that is, of standing by precedents. Stare decisis reduces legal uncertainty by enabling more confident predictions from past to future decisions. The modesty of the English judges is related to their commitment to stare decisis through the concept, or ideology, of legal positivism. Precedent is one of the sources of law

---

[50] This factor may be superficial. The English judges might have taken the position—in fact did, in the eighteenth century—that the unwritten 'British Constitution' was judicially enforceable. See Theodore F. T. Plucknett, 'Bonham's Case and Judicial Review' 40 *Harvard Law Review* 30 (1926).

[51] In 1913 the number of appellate filings was 1,515, the number of filings in the King's Bench Division 64,568, the number of county court filings 1,255,542, and the total number of first instance (i.e., non-appellate) filings 1,353,637. *Judicial Statistics, England and Wales, 1913*, pt. 2: *Civil Statistics* 9 (John Macdonell ed. 1915). These are civil filings only. The data in Table 3.3 were kindly supplied by Mr. Mark Camley of the English Court Service.

[52] Posner, note 27 above, app. A.2.

Table 3.3 English Caseloads, 1860–1994

Year	King's/Queen's Bench Division of the High Court — Writs Issued	Chancery Division of High Court — Summons Issued	Chancery Division (Bankruptcy) — Petitions Issued	County Court — Plaints Entered	Family — Divorce Petitions	Total
1860	30,778	764	2,551	782,326	293	816,712
1870	24,011	921	3,884	912,298	382	941,496
1880	53,333	953	1,831	1,095,869	662	1,152,648
1890	42,566	3,625	1,527	978,784	669	1,027,171
1900	43,784	3,441	1,459	1,180,908	611	1,230,203
1910	36,959	3,101	3,676	1,330,908	909	1,375,553
1920	44,130	2,821	1,099	457,312	4,182	509,544
1930	60,447	4,573	1,252	1,169,048	4.476	1,239,796
1940	No data were collected during the war					
1950	60,260	7.745	778	496,439	29,868	595,090
1960	57,379	5,217	699	1,489,081	28,790	1,581,166
1970	98,428	9,931	1,624	1,791,870	71,939	1,973,792
1980	200,989	7,990	6,455	1,583,901	177,415	1,976,750
1990	373,757	19,107	9,376	3,311,257	191,615	3,905,112
1991	362,564	16,577	11,522	3,694,536	179,103	4,264,302
1992	269,668	13,139	13,845	3,506,052	189,329	3,992,033
1993	211,275	10,895	13,157	3,988,828	184,471	4,408,626
1994	157,453	9,768	11,595	2,658,416	175,510	3,012,742

recognized by positivists. The judge who takes a critical view of precedent is drawing from something outside the law, as conceived by the positivist, as the basis for his critique. If he overrules a precedent (other than under the compulsion of a new statute, and then it is the legislature rather than he who is doing the overruling), he must be 'legislating'. So he had better adhere to precedent.

Even the loser-pays rule plays a role in the greater certainty of English law. It discourages the filing of novel cases, which might unsettle the law. At the same time, because English law is more certain than American law for reasons unrelated to the loser-pays rule, that rule is more 'just', and possibly more effective as a deterrent to the filing of weak cases, in England than it would be in the United States, because it is easier for an English lawyer to determine whether a claim or defense has a good chance of prevailing than it would be for an American lawyer to do so. This is a good example, incidentally, of the importance of systemic analysis and the dangers of piecemeal reform. The loser-pays rule fits the English system better than it would the American. It cannot be evaluated in the abstract (just as law cannot be defined in the abstract), but only in the setting of a specific legal system.

If certainty of legal obligation is good, and I think it is, and a causal factor in the small size of the English legal system, which it also seems to be, we should next consider whether that smaller size is a good thing in itself because resources that would otherwise be consumed in resolving legal disputes are freed up for other uses. It is like having a smaller fraction of national income devoted to national defense. But we must ask in either case whether the resources thus freed up would produce greater social value in the alternative use to which they would be likely to be put. Some would answer that reducing the size of the legal sector would increase the social product even if the resources saved by the contraction were put to no use at all. Several studies have found that the more lawyers a nation has, other things being equal, the lower its rate of economic growth.[53] Good news for England? Not really. Among their

---

[53] Kevin M. Murphy, Andrei Shleifer, and Robert W. Vishny, 'The Allocation of Talent: Implications for Growth' 106 *Quarterly Journal of Economics* 503 (1991); Samar K. Datta and Jeffrey B. Nugent, 'Adversary Activities and Per Capita

many other weaknesses,[54] the studies ignore the contributions
that lawyers make to non-market output—and non-market
output is a form of 'economic' output as economists use the
term, so it should not be ignored even by economists. The
authors assume that the major activity of lawyers is the
unproductive redistribution of wealth. But consider: the regulation of pollution is a lawyer-intensive activity the principal
outputs of which—clean air and clear water—are not included in
conventional measures of economic output. Deterring police
brutality is another non-market good that lawyers play a
significant role in producing. Likewise the deterrence of
invasions of personal privacy. Furthermore, the provision of
legal remedies is equivalent to giving the population potentially
valuable options to invoke those remedies should the need
arise. The options are separate from their exercise. People who
never in their lives bring a lawsuit may nevertheless derive
value from knowing that, should their legal rights ever be
invaded, they will be able to find a lawyer and get into court
without too much delay and with a fair chance of winning, just
as people derive utility from having fire insurance who never
have a fire. Granted, the threat of legal liability, a kind of
negative option, or tax, is also greater, the easier it is to bring a
lawsuit; and who knows how the two option values net out? All
I claim is that the proposition that increasing the number of
lawyers reduces a nation's economic growth, like the parallel
proposition no longer fashionable among economists that
advertising is socially wasteful because it is redistributive, has
not been proved. The American legal system produces more of
these equivocal options than the English system does; without

Income Growth' 14 *World Development* 1457 (1986); Stephen P. Magee, William A.
Brock, and Leslie Young, *Black Hole Tariffs and Endogenous Policy Theory: Political
Economy in General Equilibrium* 111–121 (1989). And cf. Thomas J. Campbell,
Daniel P. Kessler, and George B. Shepherd, 'The Causes and Effects of Liability
Reform: Some Empirical Evidence' (National Bureau of Economic Research
Working Paper No. 4989, Jan. 1995), finding that states that change their
products liability laws adversely to plaintiffs have higher productivity and
employment.

[54] See, for example, Charles R. Epp, 'Do Lawyers Impair Economic Growth?'
17 *Law and Social Inquiry* 585 (1992); George L. Priest, 'Lawyers, Liability, and
Law Reform: Effects on American Economic Growth and Trade Competitive-
ness' 71 *Denver University Law Review* 115 (1993).

much deeper study this cannot be thought either a good or a bad thing.

The small size of the English legal system has still another normative dimension, this one less equivocal. That small size, as we saw in Lecture One, is an indirect cause of what appears to be a lower rate of error in the English than in the American legal system.

At the high level of generality at which I have been proceeding, it is impossible to say which of the two legal systems is better on balance. English law is clearer and hence more predictable, which is a bonus but one possibly offset by a lack of flexibility (but who knows?). The English legal system is proportionately much smaller than the American, which is both a cause and an effect of the greater certainty of English law and could have an independent value if the United States has 'too many' lawyers, but again, who knows? The English have fewer rights, and have more difficulty enforcing the rights they do have, than Americans; but it is difficult to say whether on balance this is a good thing or a bad thing, since rights impose all sorts of direct and indirect costs. And English courts are less likely than American ones to make mistakes, which is a good thing and makes some rights more valuable.

Maybe we can make some progress by looking at specific areas of law.

Contract Law

An important function of a civil legal system is to facilitate productive private activities. It does this by supplying reliable remedies, not too costly to obtain, for infringements of property and contract rights and for the infliction of personal injury through negligent or otherwise unreasonable conduct. The existence of feasible remedies deters infringements and other injuries by confronting the potential violator with the threat of litigation. (In so arguing I am once again bringing deterrence to the fore in discussing civil law, as in Lecture Two.) If legal remedies are too costly relative to the likely payoff to be worth pursuing, potential wrongdoers may lack adequate incentives to avoid wrongful behavior. In that event such behavior will increase.

We can expect foreign investors and businessmen to be

especially sensitive to these concerns, since they are not obliged to invest or do business in countries other than their own. Business Environmental Risk Intelligence S.A. (BERI) is a private company that rates countries on a variety of business risks, of which one is the risk of the non-enforceability of contracts. In its current ratings BERI ranks the United Kingdom second (tied with the United States) among the 50 nations ranked, just after Switzerland, for 'Enforceability of Contracts'. Switzerland's rating (on a scale of 0 to 4) is 3.6; that of the U.K. and the U.S. is 3.5; Japan, Singapore, and the Western European countries are also in the 3's; Iran, Venezuela, and Vietnam are at the bottom, with ratings of 1.4, 1.3, and 1.4, respectively.[55] The implication is that the English legal system provides as much protection as the American, and more protection than almost any other country, for the contractual undertakings of foreigners. This is a significant vote of confidence for the English system, although it leaves open the possibility that the contractual protection of other classes of contracting parties, such as the domestic consumer, is imperfect.

Accident Cases

The *Economist* is particularly concerned about what it believes to be the patent inadequacy of English legal remedies for accidents caused by negligence.[56] This focus is lucky because the similarity of negligence law in the two legal systems enables a pretty good comparison.

'Studies show', the *Economist* tells us, 'that around 85% of accident victims . . . do not even try to claim compensation. One of the main reasons they give is fear of legal expenses.'.[57]

---

[55] The BERI rankings go back to 1972, and over this period the ratings of the United Kingdom and the United States have changed very little, and with no discernible trend. I thank Professor Stephen Knack of the Center for Institutional Reform and the Informal Sector of the University of Maryland for making these data available to me with the permission of Business Environmental Risk Intelligence S.A.

[56] Accidents that cannot be avoided by the exercise of due care are, in general, not actionable under English law. There is no compelling economic reason to make them actionable, outside of special categories (recognized in English law) of strict liability, such as strict liability for accidents resulting from abnormally dangerous activities. See William M. Landes and Richard A. Posner, *The Economic Structure of Tort Law* (1987).

[57] 'Justice in Britain' note 2 above, p. 29.

The figure is meaningless. Since accidental injuries are action-able only if the injurer was negligent, there would be no point to accident victims claiming compensation in *every* case even if the expense of doing so were much lower than it is at present. Another point the *Economist* overlooks is that the English judiciary, partly because of its small size, which facilitates the selection of able judges and encourages them to do their best (peer pressures are more effective the smaller the peer group), and partly because of its career character which I stressed in Lecture One, probably commits fewer errors in finding facts and correctly applying the law to them than the American judiciary does. The absence of the civil jury is an additional reason for thinking this, in part because the abler a legal system's judges are the less pressure there is for having juries in civil cases, where jurors are often at sea. The loser-pays rule also reduces the probability of legal error, by discouraging the filing of weak cases and the interposing of weak defenses in strong cases.

All this is important because legal error, as I have already hinted, reduces the efficacy of the threat of legal sanctions. Consider the extreme case, of liability imposed randomly. The expected liability cost of negligent behavior would be no higher than that of non-negligent behavior, and so the legal system would be providing no incentive to avoid negligence. There is a tradeoff, already alluded to, between expanding a legal system so that it can process all claims and keeping it small to minimize errors in that processing. If the relative inhospitability of the English courts to tort claims is a necessary price for minimizing the amount of error in the determination of those claims, the *net* deterrent effect of English tort law may be as great as a system of tort law that is more generous to claimants.

But let me set these points to one side and therefore assume both that many negligent English injurers are getting away with their negligence, compared with the situation in the United States, and that this effect is not offset by the fact that, for the reasons I have just explained, if a negligent injurer is sued in England he probably is more likely to lose, and if a non-negligent injurer is sued in England he probably is more likely to win, than would be the case in the United States. The assumption that many negligent injurers in England are 'getting away with it' is speculative; what is reasonably clear is that the number of negligence cases filed in English courts is disproportionately lower than in the United States. In 1986 only 51,283 personal injury suits (almost all of which would be negligence suits) were filed in English courts.[58] This was 90 per cent of all tort suits filed.[59] In contrast, 911,000 tort cases were filed in 1985 in the state and federal courts of the United States.[60] The vast majority of these—let me guess 90 per cent, similar to the English figure—would have been personal injury negligence suits. England, with roughly one-fifth the population of the United States and (as we shall see) one-half the fatal accident rate, 'should' have had one-tenth the total number of personal injury suits; it had less than one-fifteenth.

In like vein Professor Atiyah has estimated that in 1984 30 per cent of the losses of victims of automobile accidents in the United States were compensated by the tort system, compared to only 9 per cent in England, and that in 1983 there were 350 times as many products liability suits and 20 times as many suits for medical malpractice in the United States as in England.[61] Atiyah's conclusion that English accident victims are much less likely to bring tort suits than American accident victims is supported by a careful study of the claiming behavior of the two classes of victim. Before a suit is brought, the victim or his lawyer will normally make a claim against the injurer or the injurer's insurance company. English victims are less likely to do this than American victims.[62] This is what one would expect if the former are less likely to bring suit if the claim is rejected. Still another straw in the wind is a study by a management consulting firm which finds that in 1994 the cost of the English tort system, where 'cost' is broadly defined to include both legal expense and payout to claimants, was equal to only 0.8 per cent

---

[58] Lord Chancellor's Department, *Judicial Statistics, England and Wales, for the Year 1986* 25, 58 (Her Majesty's Stationary Office, Cm 9864, July 1987. 1986 is the latest year for which data are available.

[59] Id.; see also P. S. Atiyah, 'Tort Law and the Alternatives: Some Anglo-American Comparisons' 1987 *Duke Law Journal* 1002, 1010 n. 34.

[60] Kakalik and Pace, note 15 above, at 13.

[61] Atiyah, note 59 above, at 1013-1014. See also Donald Harris et al., *Compensation and Support for Illness and Injury* 327–328 (1984).

[62] Herbert M. Kritzer, 'Propensity to Sue in England and the United States of America: Blaming and Claiming in Tort Cases' 18 *Journal of Law and Society* 400 (1991).

of the English gross domestic product, compared to 2.2 per cent for the United States.[63]

Atiyah attributes the difference between the two countries in the propensity of accident victims to litigate to more generous damages awards, to substantive and procedural law more favorable to plaintiffs,[64] and to fewer alternatives to tort litigation as a method of obtaining financial compensation for injuries or other losses due to accidents, in the United States than in England.[65] England's system of socialized medicine makes it unnecessary to bring a tort suit in order to recover medical expenses incurred as the result of an accident. In other respects as well injuries and other problems that in the United States would lead to litigation tend in England to be dealt with through a variety of public mechanisms that do not involve frequent recourse to courts.[66]

In support of Atiyah's first point, the greater generosity of American than of English damages award in accident cases, I note that in 1994 in only 500 personal injury suits filed in the Queen's Bench Division was the plaintiff awarded more than £50,000 (roughly 80,000) in damages.[67] The ratio of U.S. million-dollar verdicts in tort litigation alone to equivalent verdicts in all

[63] Tillinghast-Towers Perrin, 'Tort Cost Trends: An International Perspective: 1995' 14 (1995).

[64] Among other things, class actions, a growing factor in American tort litigation, are essentially non-existent in England, because of procedural barriers summarized in J. Robert S. Prichard, 'A Systemic Approach to Comparative Law: The Effect of Cost, Fee, and Financing Rules on the Development of the Substantive Law' 17 *Journal of Legal Studies* 451, 457–458 (1988). See also John G. Fleming, 'Mass Torts' 42 *American Journal of Comparative Law* 507, 522–523 (1994).

[65] Atiyah, note 59 above, at 1019–1044. See also Franklin W. Nutter and Keith T. Bateman, *The U.S. Tort System in the Era of the Global Economy: An International Perspective* 30–39 (Alliance of American Insurers 1989).

[66] See Herbert M. Kritzer, 'The Politics of Redress: Controlling Access to the Court System in England' (University of Wisconsin-Madison, Institute for Legal Studies, Dispute Processing Research Program, Working Paper DPRP 11–6, July 1993).

[67] *Judicial Statistics, England and Wales, for the Year 1994*, note 18 above, at 32 (tab. 3.6). Corresponding figures for the county courts, where personal injury suits are also filed, are not available. But Mr. Mark Camley of the English Court Service has kindly furnished me with unpublished figures showing that in 1994, out of 668 personal injury cases tried in those courts, in only 30 were damages of more than £20,000 awarded, the average damages in those cases being £52,665. Judgments were entered in other cases, which did not go to trial, but how many and in what amount I have not been able to discover. In the Queen's Bench Division, although 950 judgments were entered in personal injury cases, only

Table 3.4 English versus U.S. Fatal Accident Rates

Type of accident	Death Rate Per 100,000 of population	
	England	United States
Motor vehicle	7.91	18.43
Other transport	0.48	1.52
Poisoning	1.43	2.33
Falls	6.37	4.95
Machinery	0.19	0.52
Fires	0.98	1.68
Firearms	0.02	0.57
Drowning	0.51	1.60
Other	2.48	5.32
Total	20.4	36.98

English cases (that is, not limited to tort cases) may be as high as 60 to 1.[68]

We might expect England to have high accident rates because of the 'inadequacy' of its tort system. Actually, as I remarked earlier, it has much lower rates. Table 3.4 compares the death rate per 100,000 population in England and the United States for the different classes of accident.[69]

I do not suggest that England has lower fatal accident rates than the United States *because* of the differences between the

330 of these were entered after trial. *Judicial Statistics, England and Wales, for the Year 1994*, note 18 above, at 30, 32 (tabs. 3.4, 3.6). This means, incidentally, that fewer than 1,000 personal injury suits were tried to judgment in England in 1994. The corresponding number for the United States is not available, but is almost certainly vastly greater. It has been estimated that in 1992 there were 20,000 tort trials in state courts. Brian J. Ostrom and Neal B. Krauder, 'Examining the Work of State Courts, 1994: A National Perspective from the Court Statistics Project' 30 (National Center for State Courts 1994).

[68] Calculated from Maimon Schwarzschild, 'Class, National Character, and the Bar Reforms in Britain: Will There Always be an England?' 9 *Connecticut Journal of International Law* 185, 218 and nn. 129–130 (1994).

[69] 1992 figures for England, 1990 figures for the United States. The source is *World Health Statistics Annual Reports*, published by the World Health Organization. The class labeled 'Machinery' also includes accidents caused by 'Cutting and Piercing Instruments'.

legal systems of the two countries; for although it is conceivable, it is very unlikely, that the absence of good legal remedies has induced potential accident victims in England to take substantially greater precautions than their American counterparts. The difference in motor vehicle and other transport fatal accident rates could be (but is not) due to differences in the amount of transportation,[70] and the difference in firearm fatal accident rates is doubtless due in large part to the far more stringent controls over the private possession of guns in England than in the United States. The point I want to make is merely that, given lower accident rates for whatever reasons, the payoff from increasing the resources devoted to controlling accidents through the legal system is likely to be less. There are many ways of controlling accidents. England seems to be highly successful in controlling them through means other than the threat of a legal sanction. The accidents that it has not been able to prevent through these other means may not be effectively deterrable by the threat of a tort suit. Maybe all the deterrable accidents have been deterred or otherwise prevented by these other means— for example by high gasoline taxes that limit driving or alter the mixture of drivers, perhaps reducing the number of young drivers, who are the most accident-prone, or by stringent gun controls. Maybe England is down to the hard core of irremediably non-deterrable—because hopelessly clumsy, foolish, crazy, or judgment-proof—injurers. Whether that is true or not, accidents do not seem to be as serious a social problem in England as in the United States. So it is not clear that devoting additional public resources to their control would be an intelligent policy, given the other claims on those resources.

I cannot exclude the possibility that the effect of awarding 'realistic' damages in English tort suits in increasing the incentive to sue would be offset, possibly more than offset, by the deterrent effect of higher damages, which by reducing the number of negligent injuries would reduce the occasions for suit. But this seems an unrealistic expectation. It is like the hope

---

[70] The death rate in automobile accidents in England is less than half that in the United States even when computed on a per mile basis—1.0 per 100 million vehicle miles driven versus 2.2 in the United States. Computed from Dept. of Commerce, Bureau of the Census, *Statistical Abstract of the United States 1992* 609 (112th ed.) (tab. 1009); *Whitaker's Almanack 1994* 513, 517 (126th ed.).

that increasing the length of prison sentences will empty the prisons by deterring people from committing crimes in the first place. In technical terms, if the elasticity of crime to a change in the severity of punishment is less than 1, an increase in that severity, while it will reduce the amount of crime, will increase the prison population.[71] Similarly, if the remaining negligent accidents in England are caused largely by a hard core of undeterrables, this implies that the elasticity of the accident rate to increases in the number of suits is less than 1 (in the limit, if the remaining negligent injurers are wholly undeterrable, it would be zero). In that event an increase in the number of suits would not be completely offset by a reduction in the number of accidents, especially if a higher proportion of the additional suits than of the existing ones would lack merit. They would. If tort law is slanted in favor of plaintiffs, and damages awards are generous, some people who are only pretending to be victims of negligent accidents will bring suit. The additional suits will have little, perhaps no, deterrent effect. They could even *reduce* the deterrent effect of tort law, as explained earlier. In this way more suits could actually beget more accidents.

If accident rates in England, though still much lower than in the United States, had been rising in recent years, this might explain the *Economist*'s concern with the small number of suits. On the contrary, according to the same statistical source, not only accident rates but the total number of accidents have been falling steadily since the mid-1950s.

I have been emphasizing deterrence but that is not the only function of a civil legal system. The system also has an insurance function to which I alluded in mentioning the option value of a legal remedy and with respect to which the American system outperforms the English, if Atiyah's estimate is correct. How important the insurance function of tort law is in light of the many alternative forms of insurance that are available may be doubted. But I am not through. The provision of a civilized substitute for private vengeance, a function distinct from either

---

[71] Elasticity is the percentage change in one variable as a consequence of a 1 per cent change in another. An elasticity of −1 would mean that a 1 per cent increase in one of the variables (say, the sentence) would cause a 1 per cent decrease in the other (say, the crime rate). In the text, I drop the minus sign.

deterrence or compensation/insurance—the function historically referred to as 'corrective justice'—remains a central function of a legal system, though no one to my knowledge believes that the English legal system is failing to perform it adequately. But even if this point is ignored along with the insurance function of a legal system—even if the deterrence of inefficient or antisocial behavior is the *only* worthwhile function of a legal system—I have not made a conclusive case against radical reform of the English legal system. I have focused on only one aspect of the civil justice system—the control of accidents. Even there I have not *proved* that providing ampler remedies for the victims of possibly negligent acts would not be worth the cost. All I have demonstrated is the difficulty of responsible evaluation of proposals for legal reform.

Another qualification—one that affects all my comparisons between English and American judicial statistics—is that it treats both countries as single units, rather than as the conglomerates they really are. This is especially questionable in the case of the United States, which is both more diverse and less centralized than England. The possibility arises that the dramatic differences that I have noted between the English and American legal systems are driven by the atypical characteristics of individual U.S. states, and hence that the differences between the 'two' systems are really differences between England and some states or regions of the United States rather than between England and the United States as a whole. The figure that I gave earlier on the number of personal injury suits filed in England in 1986 translates into 117.4 suits per 100,000 of the population. The corresponding number for the United States as a whole would have been about thrice that. But if we disaggregate, we find that in the 35 states (including the District of Columbia) in which the data are available, the number of tort suits (both state and federal) per 100,000 population ranged from 95.6 in North Dakota to 1,302.4 in Massachusetts; and one state besides North Dakota—Indiana—had fewer tort suits per 100,000 than England (111.4) and another state, Wyoming, was close (128).[72] The over-lap between English and American propensities to file

[72] The source of these data is my unpublished paper, 'Variance in the Number of Tort Suits Filed' (June 1996).

tort suits, limited as it is, suggests the possibility that the difference between the amount of tort litigation in the two countries may be in part an artifact of aggregation of the state figures. If we had a model that explained the differences in those figures in terms of variables applicable also to England, such as income, education, and urbanization, we could use it to predict the number of English tort filings; if the model overpredicted, the difference might be ascribable to features of the legal system or the broader culture. The development of such a model is an important challenge to comparative research. I do not attempt it here. But without such a model, my ascription of differences in the rate of tort suits in the two countries to differences in legal or national culture must remain highly tentative.

Criminal Cases

There is much more to a legal system than contract and tort cases. I want to glance now at some comparative data on English and American criminal cases. As I mentioned earlier, some 89,000 criminal cases were filed in the Crown Court in 1994. All of these were indictable offenses, that is, the more serious crimes, and so cannot be compared directly to the total number of criminal cases filed in American courts, 13 million in 1992,[73] of which only about 50,000 were filed in the federal courts. Some 1.5 million were felony cases filed in courts of general jurisdiction and this number[74] seems the right one to compare with the number of cases filed in the Crown Court. The disparity (almost 17 to 1 'in favor of' the United States, compared to the 5 to 1 difference in population) is particularly remarkable because, contrary to popular belief, England has a higher measured crime rate than the United States.[75] The qualification 'measured' is

---

[73] Ostrum et al., n. 33 above.

[74] Estimated from the average for the 33 states in which the number of felony cases filed in courts of general jurisdiction was reported. Id. at 39 (fig. I.57).

[75] According to Interpol's *International Crime Statistics*, in 1990 the crime rate in England and Wales was 8,986 per 100,000 of population, compared to 5,820 in the United States. The United Nations Crime Survey, which I am told is more reliable, lists 3,847,410 'serious crimes recorded' for England in 1986, compared to 13,210,800 for the United States, and obviously the second figure is not five times as large as the first. United Nations, 'Crime Trends and Criminal Justice

vital. The high level of illegal drug usage in the United States translates into an immense number of crimes that are neither reported to the police nor reported on victim-survey questionnaires. Leaving aside this point, England *seems* more law-abiding than the United States primarily because the English murder, rape, and robbery rates—the rates of the most serious crimes of violence—are far lower than those of the United States,[76] and perhaps secondarily because English crime may be more impacted.[77]

The difference in the amount and composition of criminal activity in the two countries is reflected in a comparison of all criminal prosecutions with just felony prosecutions. A vast number of English crimes are prosecuted in magistrates' courts, where the maximum prison sentence is 6 months (12 if more

Operations at the Regional and Interregional Levels' 60–61 (1993) (Annex II). Differences in the propensity to report crimes to the police can be corrected for by household surveys. The British Crime Survey estimated that 15 million crimes of all degrees of severity were committed in England (that is, England and Wales—for remember that throughout these lectures 'England' means England and Wales unless otherwise indicated) in 1991, of which 17 per cent were crimes of violence, broadly defined, and 5 per cent crimes of violence if common assaults are excluded. Pat Mayhew, Natalie Aye Maung, and Catriona Mirrlees-Black, *The 1992 British Crime Survey* 23 (Home Office Research Study No. 132, 1993). The principal U.S. victim survey came up with a count of 35 million crimes in 1991. U.S. Department of Justice, Bureau of Justice Statistics, *Criminal Victimization in the United States: 1973–92 Trends* 9 (July 1994, NCJ-147006) (tab. 1). Although the category 'all crimes' is limited to 'personal and household crimes', it appears to correspond to the 'all crimes' category in the English survey. There were 6.6 million crimes of violence according to the U.S. survey, compared to 2.55 in England that year (.17 × 15 million). If from those 6.6 million crimes of violence the 3.6 million simple assaults (id. at 39 [tab. 17]) are subtracted, the resulting figure of 3 million is still only four times greater than the corresponding English figure (.05 × 15 million = 750,000), indicating once again a higher English rate. As a final complication, however, an international study of victimization found that the probability of having been a victim of crime in the past year or five years was substantially higher in the United States than in England. Jan J. M. van Dijk, Pat Mayhew, and Martin Killias, *Experiences of Crime across the World: Key Findings from the 1989 International Crime Survey* 41, 174–175 (1990) (fig. 25 and tabs. E1, E2). This may just mean, however, that there are fewer victims of crime in England but the average English crime victim is a victim of more crimes than the average American victim.

[76] For example, in 1986 there were only 820 intentional homicides in England, compared to 20,610 in the United States. United Nations, note 75 above, at 60–61 (Annex II).
[77] The point in note 75 that a disproportionately smaller proportion of the English population may be at serious risk of being victimized.

than one offense is involved), 1,960,000 in 1993.[78] When that figure is added to the number of prosecutions in the Crown Court and compared to the total number of criminal prosecutions in the United States, 13 million, the ratio of U.S. to English prosecutions is only a little more than 6 to 1, which barely exceeds the ratio of populations, while the ratio of felony prosecutions in the United States to Crown Court prosecutions in England was, as we saw earlier, 17 to 1.

Not only does England prosecute a considerably smaller number of its serious criminals, but, partly as a consequence, it has a proportionately *much* smaller prison and jail population. In 1993 that population was only 44,565, compared to 1,392,070 in the United States.[79] The American figure is 30 times as great as the English figure, 6 times greater after correcting for the difference in the population of the two countries. This disproportion cannot be explained by reference to the higher rate of drug offenses in the United States. Subtracting prisoners convicted of or arrested for drug offenses from the U.S. total still leaves a prison and jail population of 1,049,606.[80] I do not know the percentage of drug offenders in the English prison population. But as only 3,600 out of almost 40,000 custodial sentences handed down in 1993 were for drug offences,[81] it must be small. Even if it were zero, the comparable U.S. prison population (that is excluding drug offenders) would be more than 20 times as great as the English, or 4 times on a per capita basis.

The causes of crime are complex, just like the causes of accidents. Once again it seems that England is placing less reliance on its legal system to control antisocial behavior than

[78] Home Office, *Criminal Statistics: England and Wales: 1993* 17 (Her Majesty's Stationery Office, Cm 2680, Nov. 1994).

[79] Id. at 19; Allen J. Beck and Darrell K. Gilliard, 'Bureau of Justice Statistics Bulletin: Prisoners in 1994' 1 (U.S. Dept. of Justice, Aug. 1995); Craig A. Perkins, James J. Stephan, and Allen J. Beck, 'Bureau of Justice Statistics Bulletin: Census of Jails and Annual Survey of Jails: Jails and Jail Inmates 1993–94' 1 (U.S. Dept. of Justice, April 1995).

[80] Computed from Beck and Gilliard, note 79 above, at 8, 10, 11 (tabs. 10, 13, 14), and Perkins, Stephan, and Beck, note 79 above, at 1, 14. Of course some of these are people jailed or imprisoned for drug-related crimes, such as murdering a competing drug dealer, rather than for the underlying offense. But I do not know of a responsible estimate of that figure.

[81] *Criminal Statistics: England and Wales: 1993*, note 78 above, at 155–156 (tab. 7.2).

the United States is. It may be paying a price in the form of a higher rate of criminal victimization, a term I use here to exclude victimless crimes, which appear to be much more prevalent in the United States. But the aggregate social costs of crime, as distinct from the raw crime rate, may well be lower in England because of the much lower prevalence of the crimes that cause the most fear and dislocation, as well as because of the lower prevalence of victimless crimes. As with accidents, England may be investing less in its legal system because additional investment would buy less in reducing the social cost of harmful behavior. Law is a substitute for other methods of dealing with social problems. The more effective the other methods are,[82] the less society will rely on law and so the smaller the legal system will be, whether measured by personnel or by activity.[83]

IV. NOTES TOWARD A THEORY OF LEGAL CULTURE

The title I had originally chosen for Lecture Three was 'A Theory of Legal Culture'. I discovered, however, that the formulation of such a theory was beyond my powers. Such a theory, as I envisaged it, would answer such questions as, how much of the difference between our two legal systems can be attributed to differences in ingrained modes of thought and feeling? Are the professional cultures of the two societies more alike than the two cultures as a whole, or is each professional culture a faithful mirror of the overall culture of the society (the 'national character'), or perhaps of just the intellectual culture? Is the divergence of our two legal systems—for they appear to have diverged considerably since the nineteenth century, let alone the eighteenth—a reflection of the growing apart of the two

[82] They need not be governmental methods. The much smaller demand for drugs in England than in the United States may have nothing to do with public policy in either country.

[83] David Vogel, *National Styles of Regulation: Environmental Policy in Great Britain and the United States* (1986), presents evidence that the much less contentious, adversarial, and litigious British system of environmental regulation achieves as much environmental protection as the American system. See also Robert A. Kagan, 'What Makes Uncle Sammy Run?' 21 *Law and Society Review* 717 (1988); Kritzer, note 66 above.

societies, or is it the result of developments internal to the professional culture of each society?

These are wonderfully challenging and important questions about which I have little to say. One point does occur to me, though. It has long been understood that England is a nation in which the closely related concepts of class and deference play a larger role than in the United States.[84] But it is true I think of Europe as a whole (not to mention East Asia, including Japan), and not just England, that class and deference, status and a sense of 'place', play a more important role in the organization of the society than is the case in the United States. Here may be a clue to the difference between the American legal system on the one hand and that of Europe (including England—an inclusion I insisted on in Lecture One) on the other. A deferential society is more likely to trust officials, and this has a number of implications for the legal system. To begin with, the society is apt to be more accepting of the concentration of governmental power that is characteristic of parliamentary government as opposed to the U.S.-style government of separated powers. Parliamentary government has, as we saw in Lecture One, profound implications for the judiciary. Measures designed to weaken the power of officials, such as federalism, a judicially enforceable constitution, and bicameralism and the executive veto, reduce the clarity of law and thus stimulate litigation. And judges are more likely to be trusted in a system in which officials are trusted and in which the existence of parliamentary government enables the judiciary to be thoroughly depoliticized. Trust judges, and you do not need juries as much. When English judges stopped throwing their weight around, England felt able to dispense with the civil jury. Trust non-judicial officials, and you do not need as large a legal system because people will make their complaints to officials *and* will abide by the response, as they will not do in the United States.[85]

The peculiar recruitment system traditional for English

---

[84] For an excellent discussion, see Schwarzschild, note 68 above, at 187–193.

[85] Consider in this connection the decision by the Court of Appeal to discontinue judicial review of immigration decisions. *R.* v. *Secretary of State for Home Affairs* [1986] 1 All E.R. 717 (A.C.); William Bishop, 'A Theory of Administrative Law' 19 *Journal of Legal Studies* 489, 527 (1990). That would be unthinkable in the United States.

judges, in which the judges were drawn from the ranks of the barristers and the barristers in turn were drawn from the upper class because it was so difficult to earn a living as a barrister, demonstrated the trust that the English people as a whole reposed in the upper class. Although the system of recruitment for Continental judiciaries was different, the result—an upper-class judiciary—was, I believe, similar, and helps to explain the similarity that I have emphasized between the English and Continental legal systems.

Professor Atiyah argues that the differences between the American and English rates of tort litigation can be explained without positing a greater litigiousness or quarrelsomeness of Americans than of English—can be explained simply by the pro-plaintiff slant of American tort doctrine, the more generous damages awards (including the possibility of punitive damages), and the fewer alternatives in this country for obtaining compensation for losses suffered in accidents.[86] Apparent differences in litigiousness may indeed have little or nothing to do with psychological differences, but the first two points that Atiyah emphasizes (American tort doctrine is more favorable to plaintiffs and damages awards are more generous) are merely proximate causes of differences in the rate of litigation and behind them may stand features of culture or 'national character'. 'The stereotypical images of the stoic English person and the complaining American are more than *just* stereotypes. They include a significant component of cultural representation: the American links adversity with recompense while the Englishman or woman accepts adversity as a routine part of life.'[87] The objection to agreeing with Professor Kritzer that this is an important factor in the different levels of tort claims in the two countries is that the same difference may exist between tort claiming in the United States and tort claiming in the other nations of Europe, and perhaps of the world. If the legal system of the United States is unique,[88]

---

[86] Atiyah, note 59 above.

[87] Kritzer, note 62 above, at 422.

[88] As acknowledged by Professor Galanter, the most pertinacious critic of exaggerated complaints about the litigation 'explosion' in the United States. See Mark Galanter, 'Predators and Parasites: Lawyer-Bashing and Civil Justice' 28 *Georgia Law Review* 633, 673, 677–679 (1994).

cultural differences between England and the United States are unlikely to explain the differences in the two nations' legal systems. This conclusion is consistent with my emphasis in Lecture One on the similarity between the English legal system and the legal systems of the Continent. Yet we do not, and certainly the English do not, equate the English national character to the French, Italian, or German. Indeed what is so interesting about Europe (even if we limit our consideration to Western Europe) is the extraordinary diversity of national character in so tiny and superficially homogeneous a continent. The salient English characteristics of self-restraint and non-aggressiveness[89] are not characteristic of Europeans as a whole and do appear to be plausibly related to low rates of both civil and criminal litigation. If the English rate of tort litigation is low even by European standards,[90] this would strengthen Kritzer's speculations.

Although the United States *seems* more like England than like any other European country, the American national character is virtually the opposite of the English. Deference, fatalism, self-restraint, and non-aggressiveness are just about the last characteristics that one would ascribe to Americans. Litigation is a kind of fighting, and Americans are fighters; the modern English, outside of the soccer stadium, are not. Yet I am reluctant to push 'national character' too hard as an explanation for differences in legal systems, and not only because of the sponginess of the concept. National character may be effect rather than cause, and the character of the legal system may be merely another effect of the same cause or, more realistically, the same complex of causes. The high degree of physical and social mobility in the United States, the immigrant origins of its population, its racial and ethnic heterogeneity, and the wealth and leisure of the population may be responsible for the feisty and individualistic character of the people and *independently* for a heavy demand for judicial processes of dispute resolution. A

---

[89] Well described in Daniel Snowman, *Britain and America: An Interpretation of Their Culture 1945–1975* 83–96 (1977).

[90] It appears to be much lower on a per capita basis than the German rate. See Basil S. Markesinis, 'Litigation-Mania in England, Germany and the USA: Are We So Very Different?' 49 *Cambridge Law Journal* 233, 241 (1990) (fig. 3). I have not found usable statistics for other European countries.

more static, uniform, close-knit society may simply have fewer disputes—because people understand each other better, or because the greater likelihood of continued relations or future encounters with each other puts a premium on avoiding conflict—or better informal methods of resolving disputes, though these things would not explain intra-European differences. The experience with the office of the Solicitor General of the United States, which I mentioned in Lecture One, is also some evidence that the differences in the attitude of American and English lawyers may result more from differences in incentives and constraints than from deep and mysterious cultural differences.

Political factors may be at work as well, although they too, like national character, may be epiphenomenal. One is the different orientation of the Left in England (and other European nations) and America. In England the Left is socialistic, communitarian. The entrepreneurial, lottery-style character of American litigation, with its contingent fees and class actions and giant windfall verdicts and swashbuckling multimillionaire plaintiffs' lawyers and constant harping on rights, is uncongenial to the communitarian Left. The American Left is more populist, more rights oriented, more anti-Establishment, and financed to some degree by campaign contributions from plaintiffs' lawyers.

The features of English culture, including the socialistic character of the British Labour Party, that I have been discussing are changing, although slowly, in the direction of America. At the same time there is a backlash in the United States against the perceived excesses of the American legal culture.[91] The English (if the *Economist* can be taken to reflect influential thinking in England) want to introduce the contingent fee; Americans want to curb it. Americans want to adopt the English rule (as it is called in the United States) of loser pays; the English want to move toward the American rule. In increasing the scope of appellate review of sentences (an aspect of the U.S. Sentencing Guidelines), the United States is catching up with England,

---

[91] Notable developments are the enactment of the Private Securities Litigation Reform Act of 1995, 109 Stat. 737, curtailing the rights of plaintiffs in securities litigation, and the enactment of the Antiterrorism and Effective Death Penalty Act of 1996, 110 Stat. 1214, curtailing prisoner civil rights, *habeas corpus*, and deportation litigation.

which has long had appellate review of sentences.[92] English courts have relaxed their ban on consulting legislative history as an aid to statutory interpretation,[93] while an influential current in American judicial thought urges the institution of the ban here.[94] Many Americans want to curb constitutional litigation and especially the rights of criminal defendants and prisoners; many English want to move in the opposite direction.[95] American judges are still recoiling from the perceived excesses of the Earl Warren era; English judges are flexing their muscles to a degree unprecedented since before World War I.[96]

Another area of convergence, however, may give English judicial reformers pause. English caseloads have been rising rapidly, a rise masked by my earlier use of 1913 as the benchmark. Between 1913 and 1960, the number of appeals filed actually fell by almost 20 per cent, while the number of first instance cases filed in the High Court merely doubled and the number of cases filed in the county courts increased by only about 20 per cent. Between 1960 and 1990, the number of appeals almost quadrupled (from 1,245 to 4,827), the number of first instance cases filed in the High Court more than quadrupled (from 150,984 to 664,795), and the number of cases filed in the county courts increased by almost two and a half times (from 1,492,752 to 3,561,386).[97] These increases are not so large as the corresponding increases in the U.S. federal courts, but they are large enough to cause concern, and they are doubtless part of the explanation for the erosion of the oral tradition, discussed earlier in this lecture.

---

[92] See D. A. Thomas, 'Sentencing in England' 42 *Maryland Law Review* 90, 97–115 (1983).

[93] *Pepper* v. *Hart* [1993] 1 All E.R. 42 (H.L.).

[94] See generally William S. Jordan, III, 'Legislative History and Statutory Interpretation: The Relevance of English Practice' 29 *University of San Francisco Law Review* 1 (1994).

[95] See 'Britain's Constitution: Why Britain Needs a Bill of Rights' *Economist*, 21 Oct. 1995, p. 64.

[96] For a notable example, see *Airedale National Health Service Trust* v. *Bland* [1993] 1 All E.R. 821 (H.L.), upholding the right to end the life of a vegetative accident victim. See also Stephen Sedley, 'Extra-Legal' *London Review of Books*, 19 Oct. 1995, p. 18; Anthony Lewis, 'Courts on Guard: Britain's Judges Fill a Vacuum' *New York Times*, 30 Oct. 1995, p. A15.

[97] The source of these figures is *Judicial Statistics, England and Wales*, for various years. The figures are for civil cases only.

V. LESSONS FOR THE UNITED STATES

To most American lawyers reading this book the most important question will be, are there any lessons here for us? I believe that there are several but that they do not counsel immediate, concrete changes in our system. First is simply recognition that a nation can function, perhaps even thrive, with a much smaller legal system than we have grown accustomed to. Of course, England is a poorer country than the United States. But it seems implausible to attribute the difference in wealth to the difference in legal systems. In the intangibles of life such as safety, longevity, freedom from violence, and civility—all of which are components of social welfare in a broad, but accurate, sense— England may actually be ahead of the United States.[98] The Jeremiahs who believe that the vastness, complexity, and punitiveness (both criminal and civil) of the American legal system are symptoms of dysfunction in American society rather than monuments to justice and legality may have a point, though no one seems to have a good idea of what to do about it.

Second and slightly more practical, it may be possible to reduce the burdens on American judges by institutional changes designed to place the lawyers in a more cooperative posture vis-à-vis the bench. I have suggested that in England the absence of the contingent fee, and the loser-pays rule, are among the things that operate to enlist barristers as, in effect, judicial adjuncts. We could abolish or, more realistically, tax or otherwise limit contingent fees and we could institute the English rule of loser pays. These are a natural pair, as I have said, because the loser-pays rule provides a substitute mode of financing civil litigation. Would the combination work as well in the United States as it appears to do in England? Perhaps not. American law is much less certain than English, and so it may not be realistic to expect American lawyers to do a good job of screening out marginal cases, whatever the lawyers' incentives to do so. Our fastest-growing, indeed at the moment only

---

[98] Life expectancy at birth, for example, is slightly higher in the United Kingdom than in the United States. *Human Development Report 1994*, note 14 above, at 184 (tab. 28) (1992 figures).

ominously fast-growing, caseloads are in our appellate courts,[99] and I have pointed out that the loser-pays rule may actually increase the incentive to appeal. Still, the possibility of moving a little closer to the English practice with regard to the financing of litigation deserves serious consideration, though the blocking power of the plaintiffs' bar must not be underestimated.

Bear in mind, in evaluating the desirability of reform in the system for financing litigation, that contingent-fee contracts and other 'private' arrangements involving the retention and compensation of lawyers are not indisputably Pareto-efficient market arrangements. They are sources of externalities that may warrant public intervention on non-paternalistic grounds. A contingent-fee contract alters the incentive of a lawyer to play a public role, that of judicial adjunct, for which he is not compensated by his client. Changes in the performance of that role affect the judicial system as a whole and thus other litigants. Contingent-fee contracts and rules on shifting, or not shifting, legal expenses from losing to winning parties affect the litigation rate both directly and indirectly and by doing so affect other litigants and the public generally.

A third point is one that I have not prepared the ground for, because I have not mentioned the interesting English institution of 'tribunals'. Eight of these tribunals are administered by the Lord Chancellor and deal with appeals from administrative decisions involving certain pension, transport, immigration, social security, lands, and tax matters.[100] The tribunals are themselves administrative or arbitral rather than judicial in character, and further appeal, from the decision of the tribunal to the Court of Appeal, is possible. What is striking to an American about these eight tribunals is that a system of *administrative* courts has been placed under *judicial* surveillance, the Lord Chancellor being the head of the English judiciary. It is an innovation that we might consider adopting. The better the systems of administrative appeals are, the fewer appeals are likely to be taken in administrative matters to the courts. If the same people are in charge of both the administrative and the

---

[99] A major theme of *The Federal Courts: Challenge and Reform*, note 27 above.
[100] See *Judicial Statistics. England and Wales, for the Year 1994*, note 18 above, at 73–81.

judicial courts, the former are likelier to be better managed and more 'judicial' in character, and hence better substitutes for the regular courts, than if the administrative appellate function is left to the administrative agencies themselves. To an agency its *internal* appellate function, designed as it is largely to cut down on the need for judicial review and thus save the time of judges for other matters, is likely to be of peripheral interest.

Fourth, and last, no one who studies the English legal system from the perspective of the American system can fail to be impressed by the courteous and civilized manner in which the English system manages disagreement—disagreement among judges, among barristers, and between bench and bar. No doubt this superior courtesy and civility are functions in part of the homogeneity and small size of the English bench and bar and in part of deep cultural traits of the English people. But we are not so different from the English that we cannot aspire to model our own practices on theirs where theirs are superior. Now that the 'fawning admiration often displayed by elite American lawyers for their English counterparts'[101] is a thing of the past, along with the English intelligentsia's reflex recoil from anything American, we can learn from them, and they from us. I pointed out in Lecture One that one effect of England's loser-pays rule, in contrast to the American practice of sanctioning lawyers for frivolous filings, is to reduce friction between bench and bar. It is an example of a legal rule, as distinct from an aspect of national character, that promotes civility and coopera-tion between different segments of the legal profession. Americans can learn from the English without becoming English.

---

[101] Richard L. Abel, 'The Rise of Professionalism' 6 *British Journal of Law and Society* 82, 83 (1979). See generally Richard A. Cosgrove, *Our Lady the Common Law: An Anglo-American Legal Community, 1870–1930* (1987).

Appendix A
The English Judiciary

I. AN OUTLINE OF THE COURT STRUCTURE
IN ENGLAND AND WALES*

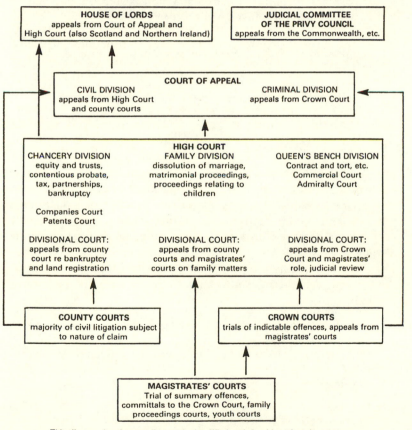

HOUSE OF LORDS
appeals from Court of Appeal and
High Court (also Scotland and Northern Ireland)

**JUDICIAL COMMITTEE
OF THE PRIVY COUNCIL**
appeals from the Commonwealth, etc.

COURT OF APPEAL

CIVIL DIVISION
appeals from High Court
and county courts

CRIMINAL DIVISION
appeals from Crown Court

HIGH COURT

CHANCERY DIVISION
equity and trusts,
contentious probate,
tax, partnerships,
bankruptcy

Companies Court
Patents Court

DIVISIONAL COURT:
appeals from county
court re bankruptcy
and land registration

FAMILY DIVISION
dissolution of marriage,
matrimonial proceedings,
proceedings relating to
children

DIVISIONAL COURT:
appeals from county
courts and magistrates'
courts on family matters

QUEEN'S BENCH DIVISION
Contract and tort, etc.
Commercial Court
Admiralty Court

DIVISIONAL COURT:
appeals from Crown
Court and magistrates'
role, judicial review

COUNTY COURTS
majority of civil litigation subject
to nature of claim

CROWN COURTS
trials of indictable offences, appeals from
magistrates' courts

MAGISTRATES' COURTS
Trial of summary offences,
committals to the Crown Court, family
proceedings courts, youth courts

This diagram is, of necessity, much simplified and should not be taken as a
comprehensive statement on the jurisdiction of any specific court

* *Source*: *Judicial Statistics, England and Wales, for the Year 1994/3* (Lord Chancellor's Department, July 1995).

II. NOTE ON THE JURISDICTION OF THE CIRCUIT JUDGE*

A. The Crown Court

1. The Crown Court has exclusive jurisdiction in trials on indictment—that is to say, the trial, at first instance, of all criminal offences which are not tried by magistrates' courts.

2. The Crown Court also sentences persons convicted by magistrates' courts but who are committed to the Crown Court because the magistrates are of the opinion that a more severe sentence may be called for than they have power to pass.

3. The Crown Court also has an appellate jurisdiction which comprises mainly appeals from magistrates' courts in criminal matters and youth court proceedings, but also includes some appeals in civil matters. The most important such appeals are those in relation to licensing and betting and gaming cases.

4. In the Crown Court, cases are classified into 4 classes under directions made by the Lord Chief Justice. Those in classes 1 and 2 are nominally reserved for trial by High Court Judges. In class 1, however, many cases of murder, or of incitement, attempt or conspiracy to commit murder, are in practice tried by authorised Circuit Judges, whilst in class 2, the great majority of offences, other than piracy, mutiny, sedition and offences under the Geneva Convention, are tried by authorised Circuit Judges. Class 2 includes most serious sexual offences, along with manslaughter and child destruction.

5. The majority of fraud cases are tried by Circuit Judges; some may be allocated to High Court Judges.

6. All other offences are either automatically listed for trial by Circuit Judges or Recorders or are normally so listed unless a particularly difficult case is specially reserved for trial by a High Court Judge. When trying a case in the Crown Court, the Circuit Judge has the full range of powers, by way of sentence or otherwise, fixed by statute or at common law, in relation to particular offences.

7. In relation to indictable offences, the right of appeal lies against conviction or sentence from the Crown Court to the Criminal Division of the Court of Appeal, subject to leave unless the appeal

* *Source*: *Developments in Judicial Appointments Procedures* 14–16 (Lord Chancellor's Department, May 1994).

is solely on a point of law. The right of appeal in appellate matters lies by way of case stated to the Divisional Court of the Queen's Bench Division except in relation to certain matters such as licensing, where the decision of the Crown Court is final.

B. *The County Courts*

8. The jurisdiction of the county courts is entirely statutory and covers almost the whole field of civil and family law. The general jurisdiction in civil law is mostly concurrent with that of the High Court.

9. A number of statutes confer exclusive jurisdiction on the county courts. These cover important areas of work of the county courts, for example virtually all cases under the Consumer Credit Act, actions by mortgage lenders for possession and actions by landlords under the Rent Acts and the Housing Acts 1985 and 1988.

10. Since 1 July 1991 the concurrent jurisdiction has been substantially increased by orders made under the Courts and Legal Services Act 1990. In common law cases, basically tort including personal injuries, debt and other breaches of contract, there is no monetary limit on the jurisdiction of the county courts but cases with a value greater than £50,000 will normally be heard in the High Court and cases with a value below £25,000 will normally be heard in the county courts. Straightforward cases between these two limits will also normally be determined in the county courts.

11. In equity proceedings the monetary limit is currently £30,000. In cases involving land, county courts have jurisdiction where the rateable value at 31 March 1990 did not exceed £1,000 or £1,500 in Greater London. The county courts have unlimited jurisdiction in applications under the Inheritance Act 1975 and s. 30, s. 146 and s. 147 of the Law of Property Act 1925. In Companies Act cases the jurisdiction covers cases where the total paid up share capital of the company is less than £120,000.

12. In addition to the general jurisdiction, about 80 per cent of county courts have jurisdiction in insolvency, and some county courts have admiralty jurisdiction in relation to claims up to £5,000 (£15,000 in salvage claims). A few Circuit Judges in a small number of courts also exercise specialist jurisdictions under, for example, the Race Relations Act 1976.

13. In family law the jurisdiction is similarly divided either by statute or practice direction. In some matters, such as adoption, the county

courts have concurrent jurisdiction with the High Court. In other matters, county courts have exclusive jurisdiction, e.g., virtually all divorce proceedings.

14. The county courts share jurisdiction with the High Court and the Family Proceedings Court in applications under the Children Act 1989, the work being dealt with at the appropriate level pursuant to allocations directions. In the county courts where such applications relate to public law cases such as care and supervision orders they are heard by designated Circuit Judges sitting at Care Centres and all directions in such matters are dealt with by designated District Judges sitting at the Care Centres.

C. The High Court

15. In addition to the concurrent jurisdiction of the county courts and the High Court mentioned above, under s. 9 of the Supreme Court Act 1981, a Circuit Judge may be invited to sit as a judge of the High Court to provide flexibility in the disposal of High Court business. Where a Circuit Judge sits in the High Court he or she possesses all the powers of a High Court Judge.

III. NOTE ON THE JURISDICTION OF A DISTRICT JUDGE*

A. County Court Jurisdiction

1. The jurisdiction of the county courts is entirely statutory and covers almost the whole field of civil and family law. The general jurisdiction in civil law is mostly concurrent with that of the High Court.

2. A number of statutes confer exclusive jurisdiction on the county courts. These cover important areas of work of the county courts, for example virtually all cases under the Consumer Credit Act 1974, actions by mortgage lenders for possession and actions by landlords under the Rent Acts and the Housing Acts 1985 and 1988.

3. Since 1 July 1991 the concurrent jurisdiction has been substantially increased by orders made under the Courts and Legal Services Act 1990. In common law cases, basically tort including personal

---

* *Source*: *Developments in Judicial Appointments Procedures* 26–30 (Lord Chancellor's Department, May 1994).

injuries, debt and other breaches of contract, there is no monetary limit on the jurisdiction of the county courts but cases with a value greater than £50,000 will normally be heard in the High Court and cases with a value below £25,000 will normally be heard in the county courts. Straightforward cases between these two limits will also normally be determined in the county courts.

4. In equity proceedings the monetary limit is currently £30,000. In cases involving land, county courts have jurisdiction where the rateable value at 31 March 1990 did not exceed £1,000 or £1,500 in Greater London. The county courts have unlimited jurisdiction in applications under the Inheritance Act 1975 and s. 30, s. 146 and s. 147 of the Law of Property Act 1925. In Companies Act cases the jurisdiction covers cases where the total paid up share capital of the company is less than £120,000.

5. In family law the jurisdiction is similarly divided either by statute or practice direction. In some matters, such as adoption, the county courts have concurrent jurisdiction with the High Court. In other matters, county courts have exclusive jurisdiction, e.g., virtually all divorce proceedings.

6. The county courts share jurisdiction with the High Court and the Family Proceedings Court in applications under the Children Act 1989, the work being dealt with at the appropriate level pursuant to allocations directions. In the county courts where such applications relate to public law cases such as care and supervision orders they are heard by designated Circuit Judges sitting at Care Centres and all directions in such matters are dealt with by designated District Judges sitting at the Care Centres.

B. Jurisdiction of the District Judge

This can conveniently be considered (for the purposes of this note only) under four main headings viz: the general jurisdiction of the county courts; special jurisdiction of the county courts; county court family jurisdiction; and High Court jurisdiction.

General Jurisdiction of the County Courts

1. In the county courts, District Judges have general power to try any action where the amount claimed does not exceed £5,000. When trying such actions, they have all the powers of the court including those relating to injunctions and specific performance but with only limited powers to deal with contempt of court. When assessing damages the jurisdiction of the District Judge is unlimited.

2. With the consent of the Circuit Judge and the parties they may also try any action in the county courts.

3. Where the case is undefended or where only one party appears at the hearing, they may exercise all the powers of the Circuit Judge except committal for contempt of court.

4. They deal with all interlocutory matters and pre-trial reviews.

5. They may be and frequently are required finally to dispose of an action either by giving summary judgment for the plaintiff or by dismissing a claim which discloses no cause of action or where a party has been guilty of inexcusable delay in prosecuting the action.

6. They have power to order interim payments on account of damages claimed by the plaintiff.

7. District Judges hear most actions for possession. They have unlimited jurisdiction over any money claim which is included in a possession action. All of these possession actions involve the exercise of a judicial discretion in deciding whether a possession order should be made and, if so, the terms (if any) upon which the enforcement of the order should be suspended.

8. District Judges acts as arbitrators in all cases referred to arbitration and these now form a substantial and important part of the work of the county courts. Upon filing a defence, claims are automatically referred to arbitration where the amount of the claim does not exceed £1,000. Other claims over £1,000 may be referred to arbitration on the application of either party to the proceedings. In 'automatic' arbitrations limited costs only are normally awarded and parties are encouraged to dispense with legal representation.

9. In relation to costs, they exercise all the powers of a Taxing Master of the Supreme Court in deciding without any monetary limit, the reasonableness of the sums claimed for costs in actions where an order is made in the county courts for payment of costs by one party to another.

10. In cases where a party is legally aided, they are effectively the sole arbiters of the proper amount which the solicitor and barrister are entitled to receive.

11. They also have jurisdiction to determine the reasonableness of costs charged by a solicitor to his or her own client in respect of litigation in the county courts, where the amount of the bill does not exceed £5,000.

12. They decide most questions arising from the enforcement of county court judgments. These include disputed applications to suspend possession warrants and warrants of execution; applications for charging orders and for the sale of property subject to a Charging Order; and applications for garnishee orders and attachment of earnings orders made by the court staff, where the order is disputed, and all applications to enforce maintenance payments by attachment of earnings.

13. Where damages are recovered by a person under disability, for example a minor, they are responsible for approving the terms of any settlement of the proceedings. They also decide how the money is to be invested or dealt with for the benefit of that person, for example by approving the terms of a private trust, by the use of the various forms of investment available through the Court Funds Office, or by immediate payment out.

14. District Judges have power to fine or commit to prison any person who disobeys orders made under the Attachment of Earnings Act 1971, any person who assaults any officer of the court, or any person who wilfully misbehaves in the court, and to fine or commit any person who refuses to give evidence to the court.

Special Jurisdiction of the County Courts

1. In addition to the general jurisdiction, about 80 per cent of county courts have jurisdiction in insolvency and the District Judges sitting at these courts exercise all the power of the Bankruptcy Registrars of the Supreme Court in dealing with personal insolvency.

2. District Judges also have power to deal with winding up of companies where the total paid up share capital of the company is less than £120,000.

3. These powers include the power to order the arrest of individuals and company officers in default and the power to disqualify company directors from office for up to ten years.

4. Some county courts have admiralty jurisdiction in relation to claims up to £5,000, £15,000 in salvage claims. Some District Judges sitting at these courts have power to give directions including ordering the arrest and release of any ship or aircraft.

County Court Family Jurisdiction

1. The Children Act 1989, implemented in October 1991, allocated new responsibilities to District Judges in family proceedings. All District Judges at county courts with divorce jurisdiction have

jurisdiction in private law family matters. This includes divorce (see below) and giving directions for a range of orders (s. 8 orders) concerning the child's upbringing, both after divorce and in freestanding applications. They can also make uncontested s. 8 orders and interim orders for residence and contact in contested cases; vary a s. 8 order when a family assistance order is in force. They set the timetable and exercise the control of the court over such applications.

2. Some Nominated Care District Judges automatically have jurisdiction in public law family matters. This includes reviewing refusals by Family Proceedings Courts to transfer cases to county courts or the High Court; making Emergency Protection Orders for children at risk; and making unopposed orders for care and supervision. They can make opposed interim care and supervision orders.

3. Under the special procedure which applies to undefended divorce cases, the District Judge has to consider the petition and affidavit in support, certify whether a decree may be granted and pronounce it in open court. He or she also has to consider the arrangements for any minor children of the family either by consideration of the documentary evidence as to the arrangements or by hearing from the parties at an appointment.

4. District Judges have unlimited jurisdiction to deal with all questions relating to property and spousal maintenance pending and after divorce. The Matrimonial Causes Act 1973 confers the widest possible discretion upon the court to adjust both the income and capital of the parties to a divorce. Applications for financial provision are finally determined by the District Judge. These applications are a heavy and important part of the work undertaken by District Judges. Hearings can run over several days and the value of the property in dispute can be substantial.

5. Within financial applications District Judges also have power to grant injunctions restraining parties from disposing of matrimonial assets and to set aside transactions undertaken to defeat a claim for financial relief.

6. Under the Matrimonial Homes Act 1973, District Judges have the power to make orders for the transfer of a tenancy from one spouse to the other and orders terminating or suspending rights of occupation in the matrimonial home. All District Judges may hear applications for matrimonial injunctions (e.g., non-molestation or ouster orders) but they may not commit for breach of such an order.

7. All District Judges at divorce courts may give directions in adoption cases.

High Court Jurisdiction

1. Except in those matters expressly reserved to the county courts or to special Tribunals, the High Court exercises an unlimited jurisdiction in all civil matters. With the exception of a very few matters, which rarely arise in practice, any High Court action may be begun in a District Registry, proceeding to trial either in London or at one of the other trial centres where High Court proceedings are dealt with.

2. The jurisdiction of the District Judge in High Court Queen's Bench proceedings covers all interlocutory matters including interrogatories, discovery and amendment and particularisation of pleadings. In addition to the unlimited amount of the claim, applications for summary judgment or to strike out a claim may involve difficult and highly technical arguments on points of law and pleading.

3. In addition, they have power to hear applications for renewal of writs and applications to extend the time limits for commencement of proceedings under the Limitation Act 1980.

4. They have power to make final assessments of damages, without any monetary limit.

5. When a case is set down for trial, they are responsible for reviewing the action in order to determine whether it is of sufficient importance to remain in the High Court or whether it should be transferred down to the county courts.

6. A few District Registries in the largest conurbations have full Chancery jurisdiction and District Judges at these centres exercise all the powers of a Chancery Master of the High Court in London.

7. In relation to costs, District Judges exercise all the powers of a Taxing Master of the Supreme Court in all cases proceeding in the District Registry and over any costs charged by a solicitor to his or her own client.

8. With the coming into force of the Children Act 1989 the wardship jurisdiction has substantially reduced although it remains available in appropriate cases. District Judges hear the first appointment giving all necessary directions to enable the case to proceed to trial and are responsible for ensuring that it is tried without any unnecessary delay.

Appendix B

I. THE UDU CASE

When I was in England to deliver the Clarendon Lectures I spent a part of one day watching arguments in the Court of Appeal. One case that I watched struck me as a particularly clear illustration of the English judicial method, superficially so like the American yet fundamentally so different. I want first to describe the setting. The appellate courtrooms in the Royal Courts of Justice (recently renovated) in London (the Court of Appeal sits only in London) are small by American standards and rather austerely furnished and decorated, though not at all shabby. But the judges' bench is more elevated than in an American courtroom, making the English courtroom at once more intimate and more hierarchical, more cozy and more formal, than the American. The judges and barristers are of course wigged, and it is the custom for people entering or leaving the courtroom to bow slightly to the bench. These touches reinforce the formality of the proceeding. Yet there is less tension, less adversariness than in an American courtroom. The temperature is lower. An atmosphere of perfect courtesy prevails. The barristers do not bluster, or the judges eye them with suspicion.

The *Udu* case that I am about to describe was unusual because there was only one barrister, the respondent not having bothered to appear. Udu had applied to the governing council of the municipality where he lives, the London Borough of Southwark, for a grant to enable him to take a one-year course at a proprietary law school that would enable him to qualify as a solicitor. The borough turned him down on the basis of its policy of not making grants for study in proprietary institutions. Udu complained that the policy was unreasonable because there are not enough places in the non-proprietary solicitors' schools and he could not afford the fee of the proprietary school. His barrister, a young man, had submitted a 'skeleton argument', which is to say a brief outline of his arguments, not a brief in the American sense. The barrister argued for about half an hour. The presiding judge, Lord Justice Staughton, asked many questions, directing the barrister to the issues that concerned the three-judge panel. The statute empowering the borough to make educational grants (but setting forth no criteria for the exercise of the power) was handed up to the judges to read during the argument. At the conclusion the judges retired for no more than five minutes, then returned to the bench, and the presiding judge, speaking without pauses, dictated an opinion, turning down Udu's appeal. A transcript of the oral opinion was submitted to the judge, who made minute corrections, limited almost entirely to punctuation (the stenographer's contribution). I print the edited transcript below. When one considers that the judges' exposure to the case consisted essentially of a half hour argument by a barrister with no briefs, no adversary presentation, no assistance from law clerks, and no time for extended reflection, the performance of the presiding judge in extemporizing this elegant and comprehensive opinion is remarkable by American standards, though I believe fairly typical of the Court of Appeal. It reflects the career character of the English judiciary (Lord Justice Staughton's entire career having been spent as a barrister and a judge), the relation of trust between bench and bar (the court could trust Udu's barrister to furnish it with all the materials relevant to decision even though there was no opposing barrister to keep Udu's barrister honest), and the greater simplicity of English law. American judges jump through elaborate conceptual hoops in deciding whether to sustain an administrative decision, such as the denial of a grant. The Court of Appeal was content to consider the issue one simply of reasonableness.

CO/3366/94

IN THE SUPREME COURT OF JUDICATURE
COURT OF APPEAL (CIVIL DIVISION)
ON APPEAL FROM THE HIGH COURT OF JUSTICE
(DIVISIONAL COURT (CROWN OFFICE)
On application for leave to appeal)

Royal Courts of Justice
Friday, 27th October 1995

Before:

LORD JUSTICE STAUGHTON
LORD JUSTICE HENRY
and
LORD JUSTICE PILL

_____

THE QUEEN

—v—

LONDON BOROUGH OF SOUTHWARK
Ex parte OCHUKO UDU

_____

MR. P. DIAMOND (instructed by Messrs J.R. Jones, London, W5)
appeared on behalf of the Applicant.

THE RESPONDENT did not appear and was not represented.

_____

JUDGMENT
(As Approved by the Court)

© Crown Copyright

LORD JUSTICE STAUGHTON: Ochuko Udu lives in the London Borough of Southwark. He has obtained a law degree in Class 2.1 at Southwark University. He has been offered a place on the Legal Practice course at the College of Law, Guildford, but he needs money to pay the course fees and to support himself. He has applied to the Council of the London Borough of Southwark for a grant, but they have refused. He appealed against that refusal, again to the Council, and his appeal was turned down. He has sought leave to apply for judicial review of the Council's decision. His application came before Laws J., and it was dismissed. Thus he makes a renewed application in this court today.

First of all, the legislation. Section 2 of the Education Act 1962, substituted by the Education Act 1980, provides in subsection (1):

'A local education authority shall have power to bestow awards on persons over compulsory schools age (including persons undergoing training as teachers) in respect of their attendance at courses to which this section applies and to make such payments as are payable in pursuance of such awards.'

Subsection (2) says that:

'. . . this section applies to any course of full-time or part-time education . . . which is not a course of primary or secondary education . . .'

and is not in section 1. Section 1, by contrast to section 2, provides for a mandatory grant for students who go to college or university for a first degree, in broad terms.

So the London Borough of Southwark had a discretion whether to make a grant to Mr. Udu for his legal practice course. The reasons which they gave for refusing a grant were as follows:

'Awards are normally restricted to students wishing to obtain recognised qualifications at establishments maintained out of public funds and awards are not, therefore, available to students wishing to pursue their studies at private colleges or universities.'

There was another reason given a little later, I suspect in connection with the appeal:

'The Council has a general policy not to assist students who wish to attend private colleges nor to assist students taking postgraduate level courses. However, it is always prepared to consider exceptional cases.'

Both those reasons were an obstacle for Mr. Udu, because the Legal Practice Course is a postgraduate level course.

The Council are perfectly entitled to have a policy. Fairness, after all, demands that like cases should be treated alike, and the policy will promote that objective. But it is also right that the Council should be prepared to depart from their policy if there are special circumstances. The letter said that they do do that. This Council has £511,000 in one year for discretionary grants. I do not suppose that that is enough for all the applications from young people in Southwark, by a long chalk.

Can the Council properly exclude privately funded institutions? The College of Law is not the only avenue to becoming a solicitor nowadays. There are other institutions which are publicly funded which teach that course. But more than half of the students go to the College of Law. The publicly funded institutions, Mr. Udu says, become very quickly filled up. The Council is a political body and the decision not to give grants to students going to privately funded institutions is a political decision. It is not for us to criticise it.

Can the Council properly exclude postgraduate courses? They may take the view that young people, who have already had the benefit of a grant for their first degree, have had their share of assistance from the Council's budget. That is a view which they can logically take. For many years now, some Councils have been refusing to give grants for aspiring lawyers, whether they want to be barristers or solicitors. This has not been held to be illegal.

Mr. Udu says that if the Southwark policy is upheld, the legal profession will become entirely filled with the affluent or, at any rate, the children of the affluent. It would follow, although he is good enough not to say this, that judges would become even more out of touch with ordinary people than they are already. It is not only Mr. Udu who has this concern. The Law Society have expressed it in a study they have made of the legal profession. It is called *Entry into the Legal Profession* and it is *Research Study No. 15*, where they say:

'It is arguable that the only reason why the present system has been sustainable is because of the unusually affluent backgrounds of those students who apply to do law in the first place.'

I am afraid that that may be so. Of course, some students may be able to find part-time jobs to support themselves during further education, as happens commonly in the United States. Some students may obtain assistance from the Inns of Court if they wish to become barristers or from solicitors' firms if they want to qualify as solicitors. But not all will be able to obtain help by those routes. Whether the remainder should have grants is a matter for the Local Education Authority. Schiemann J. in the case of *R. v. Warwickshire County Council, ex parte Williams* (unreported) said that:

'. . . local authorities should be free to decide, each according to its own local sense of priorities, how much to spend on discretionary awards including a freedom to decide to spend very little indeed if anything.'

I would not in this case rule that this is inevitably the right answer to this problem. But it seems to me that it was well within the discretion of the London Borough of Southwark to reject the application in this case for the reasons that it did.

Mr. Diamond has relied on the debate in the House of Commons Committee when the Education Act 1962 was under consideration. The passage he read to us from Hansard seemed to me to be not of great assistance to his cause. There was an amendment to section 2 proposed by one Member of the Committee which would have made the grants under that section mandatory as they were under section 1 (Hansard, 5th December 1961, columns 187, 188 and 190). The amendment was not accepted. It was in fact rejected, so that there is no support there for the notion that the Council was under any duty to make this grant. We were also referred to the Anderson report, which preceded the Education Act 1961, and a Circular issued by the Minister as to how he hoped local authorities would administer their discretion under section 2. I am afraid that none of that material assists Mr. Udu's cause. In my judgment, this application must be refused.

LORD JUSTICE HENRY: I agree.

LORD JUSTICE PILL: I also agree.

Application dismissed with legal aid taxation
of the applicant's costs

Index